Live Well.

Be Happy.

28 Lessons to Help You Stay Sane
& Balanced in a Crazy World

Richard De A'Morelli

Spectrum Ink Publishing
Morro Bay, California

Live Well. Be Happy.

Copyright © 2017, 2019 by Spectrum Ink Publishing

Published simultaneously in Canada & the United States
First Edition: January, 2017
Second Edition: August, 2019

Previously released in 2015 as *You Can Change Your Life*, this edition has been extensively revised, new material added, and retitled to avoid confusion with other similarly titled works.

No part of this book may be reproduced or transmitted by any means including photocopying, recording, taping, or digital reproduction, or posted on any blog or website without the publisher's knowledge and consent except for brief quotations embodied in critical articles and reviews.

Cover photograph licensed from Adobe Stock Graphics. All rights reserved.

ISBN numbers:
978-0-993634-09-3 : Kindle/Mobi (digital)
978-0-993634-08-6 : Epub (digital)
978-0-993634-04-8 : Paperback (Amazon)
978-0-993636-46-9 : Paperback (Ingram Retail/Wholesale)
978-1-988236-40-7 : Hardcover (Ingram Retail/Wholesale)

Spectrum Ink Publishing
Morro Bay, California

Editorial/Distribution:
1-805-888-2900

Website:
https://books.spectrum.org/

DEDICATION

This book is dedicated to the loving memory of my son, David.

Other Books by Richard De A'Morelli

- *Elements of Style 2017: A Grammar, Style, and Punctuation Handbook for Modern Writers*
- *Elements of Style: Classic Edition (2018)*
- *Elements of Style Grammar Workbook*
- *Quick & Easy English Punctuation*
- *As a Man Thinks: Classic Edition (Editor)*

For details on these books and ordering information, please visit https://books.spectrum.org

To contact Richard De A'Morelli directly, visit his virtual office at https://richard.spectrum.org/

A Message from the Publisher

We hope you enjoy reading this book. Good reviews help spread the word to others about the books you find useful. Please take a minute to post a review at your favorite online bookseller. Even a sentence or two will be greatly appreciated!

Subscribe to Our Mailing List

Subscribe to our free newsletter and be among the first to learn about new books from Richard De A'Morelli and other Spectrum Ink authors, as well as discount coupons, contests, and more. Sign up at https://books.spectrum.org/subscribe.html

Table of Contents

PART I: Change Your Life
Lesson 1: Your Life Story, Your Choices 9
Lesson 2: Breaking Free of the Past 13
Lesson 3: Your Blueprint for Change 21
Lesson 4: Relax, Breath, and Start Living 33
Lesson 5: The Courage to Change Your Life 39
Lesson 6: Visualize the Possibilities 47
Lesson 7: Creating Your Own Destiny 51

PART II: Share the Light
Lesson 8: Wisdom Is Knowledge Applied 59
Lesson 9: Make Every Day Count 61
Lesson 10: Seeking the Spiritual 65
Lesson 11: A Fork in the Road 77
Lesson 12: Finding Your Strength Within 81
Lesson 13: Acts of Kindness in Daily Life 83
Lesson 14: Letting Go and Starting Over 85
Lesson 15: The Courage to Conquer Fear 89
Lesson 16: Calming Mind, Body, and Spirit 93
Lesson 17: Stress—How to Cope With It 97
Lesson 18: The Power of Mantra Meditation 105
Lesson 19: Centering in the Here and Now 109
Lesson 20: Something Beautiful for God 111
Lesson 21: Conflict Resolution 115
Lesson 22: The Art of Creating Happiness 117
Lesson 23: Support: It Really Does Matter 119
Lesson 24: The Power of Validation 121
Lesson 25: I Changed My Life—So Can You! 123
Lesson 26: The Secret Power of Dreams 125
Lesson 27: Making Choices 129
Lesson 28: Out From the Heart 131
About the Author 155
More Books from Spectrum Ink 157

Part I
Change Your Life

Lesson 1

Your Life Story, Your Choices

Life in this 21st century world is complicated, confusing, and stressful. Social norms are in flux, the world is in turmoil, families and friends are divided by politics and religion, and the news is filled with disturbing headlines. At the same time, technology has advanced with leaps and bounds. The Internet has become a second home for millions who socialize, learn, shop, and date online. It's astonishing how much the world has changed just in the past thirty years, and as a consequence, our lives have become ever more complicated as the winds of progress and change continue to blow all around us.

With so much stress and uncertainty affecting us in day-to-day living, it is more important than ever to find ways to stay sane, positive, and focused on what matters most to us. In this book, you will learn methods you can use to remain balanced and keep a positive perspective in life, even when drama and chaos are erupting all around you. You can't control the thoughts or actions of people causing you aggravation, but how you react to them is your choice. You can let yourself be drawn into drama and discord, or you can remain above the fray and not be a willing participant in the games people play.

That's an important point to remember: You choose how you react to others. In fact, life is all about making choices. Whether you make decisions based on careful thought, force of habit, subconscious motivations, or impulse, everything that has happened in your life has been a result of the choices you've made. Likewise, the choices you make today will plant the seeds in the spiritual garden that awaits you in the future. Tomorrow will become the present, and today's choices will add bricks and mortar to the foundation of your past. Make the right decisions, take the right actions, and wonderful things will happen in your life.

But wait! What about situations in the past where you made no decision—things just happened? Sometimes it's difficult to see the cause-and-effect link between a decision and its outcome, especially when you didn't actually make a choice. But procrastination, delay, and inaction are choices—you decide, consciously or without realizing it, to do nothing. Perhaps you are unsure of the right course of action; maybe the outcome you expect won't be to your liking. Or you might hope that if you ignore a situation, it will go away. It won't; and choosing to do nothing usually makes it worse. When you choose inaction, you surrender control over the outcome to someone else. That person will almost always opt for what is best for him, and your welfare will be secondary or of no concern. You can probably recall unpleasant situations that came about because you put off a decision and someone else made it for you.

You are who you are today because of your past. It has shaped and molded your character and temperament, your attitudes and desires, your approach to relationships and life in general, and the very foundation of your hopes and dreams for the future. Your choices are the building blocks of your past.

We're often told that we should live in the present or "in the moment." But the present only lasts for an instant, and then it becomes the past. The elusive quality of time, where the future morphs into the present and fades into the past as the universal clock ticks on is summed up well by the saying: *Today is the tomorrow you worried about yesterday.*

As much as you might want to rewrite pages of your life story in the past, they can't be changed. The ink has dried. There's only the present and the future—and the present is elusive because, by the time you finish writing today's entry in your life journal, it is yesterday's news. Only the pages of the future remain blank. Only you can write on them. And what you write will depend on the choices you make and actions you take in the here and now. Today. Tomorrow. The next day. And in the weeks to come. Will the life story you write be a sad tale of unwise choices, lost opportunities, self-destructive habits, and failure? Or will it be a happy story filled with love and light, laughter, success, wellness, caring friends, devoted family, and a bright spiritual destiny? It's your story, your plot, and your choices.

By reading the first few pages of this book, it's safe to assume that you are at least wondering if it's possible for you to live well and be happy. That's a first step; and, yes, it certainly is possible. But you'll need to make a few choices—and that's why I opened with a lesson on that very topic! First and foremost, you need to decide that you want to live well and be happy. It has to be a conscious decision. It won't happen randomly when you wake up one morning. Then, you will need to make a few more choices and take actions to help you stay sane, positive, and balanced in everyday life. You may need to adjust some of your attitudes; for instance, realize that bitter arguments with family or friends is a drain on your time and emotional energy. Rather than fighting, you can learn simple methods described in this book to deal with those who annoy you— neutralize their influence; use subtle means to coax them to your point of view; learn to understand and respect their views; or tune them out.

In the following chapters, you will learn how to tap into the limitless power of the human mind and use this powerful force to change your life. You will discover ways to reduce stress, overcome depression, and avoid conflicts with your family, friends and colleagues at work. We will discuss simple methods you can use to stay balanced in day-to-day living such as deep relaxation, visualization, rhythm breathing, and meditation; and you will learn effective ways to build confidence and replace self-destructive habits with healthy behavior. The book also touches on how to deal with seeds of karma planted in your spiritual garden long ago, and how you can bring positivity and light into your life and to those you care about.

All that we have in this physical world is the time allotted to us, and it is a precious gift. You have a limited number of years, months, weeks, and days, in your life. You can guesstimate how much time you might have left, but life is never predictable. In the end, all that will matter when you look back on your life is: Did you live well? Were you happy? Did you bring happiness to others? Will you leave your corner of the world a better place than when you came into it? How you answer those questions will be shaped by your thoughts and actions today, tomorrow, and in the days to come.

Learn how to live well. Learn how to be happy. Everything else in your life is connected and will fall into place.

Lesson 2

Breaking Free of the Past

I have spent a lot of time dwelling on the past lately. Tragedy and loss can drive even the most optimistic and spiritual people to despair. The loss of a child is terribly painful; and when that child is your only child, the paralyzing grief that sets in is beyond words. It's easy for others to say: "Leave the past behind and move on with your life." But it's not easy or even possible to follow that advice when the wounds from a tragedy are fresh and emotions are raw. Instead, one retreats into memories of happier times and becomes a prisoner of the past.

I have believed in the law of cause of and effect, which is known by various names, since I was introduced to the concept at age ten. It's an obvious law of nature: Every action produces a reaction. When you toss an apple in the air, it comes down. Throw a stone in a pond and it creates ripples. When you make wrong choices in life, those actions produce reactions, and we call them consequences. We might not know until later whether a choice is the correct one, or whether it will have consequences. Sometimes, it takes years or a lifetime for actions to come full circle before we find out.

From the age of twelve, I felt a compelling urge to be a writer, though looking back, I never understood why. I published my first article in a national magazine soon after I turned fourteen. A few months later, I ran away from home to escape an abusive parent. I grew up on the streets, and life wasn't easy. Being a ninth-grade dropout, I knew my prospects for success as a freelance writer were dim; but I was determined and stubborn. I taught myself the basics of grammar, spelling, and punctuation. The summer after I turned eighteen, a paperback publisher offered me a book contract.

Over the next decade, I published a dozen books the old-school way—Amazon.com and its self-publishing platform were years off in the future, and the only way to have a book published was to write better than anyone else and find a publisher willing to gamble thousands of dollars on printing and storing paper books in a warehouse. I was fortunate to have landed a multi-book contract, and I devoted the following years to writing inspirational books, teaching classes on psychic development and meditation, and enjoying a bit of fame at the top of my field. My wife at the time laughed with delight when she went to the supermarket and saw my photo, at least once a month, on the front page of *The Star* under the headline "World's Top Ten Psychics Predict..."

It was a bright summer day when I received a call from a woman named Carole who identified herself as the senior editor for Irving Wallace, one of the world's bestselling authors at the time. She offered me a writing gig. I would contribute to Wallace's popular *Book of Lists* and *Book of Predictions* series, and I would receive by-lined credit as a member of his editorial staff plus more money than I had ever earned as a freelance writer. I practically shouted, "Yes! Of course! I accept!" It was the opportunity of a lifetime for a struggling writer. I was convinced that fate had smiled down on me and my future was bright. I would soon discover how quickly a sunny life outlook can change.

One afternoon a few weeks later, I was watching news on TV and a story came on about a young boy who had been reported missing by his mother in a town about a ninety-minute drive to the south. Unexpectedly, a series of gruesome images flashed through my mind. As the scene played out like a video with no Stop button, I saw a man beating the boy, and then I saw him bury the child in a field. I sensed that the man was the boy's father or stepfather. A woman stood nearby, crying, and I sensed that she was the mother. I was depressed for the rest of the evening and spent a sleepless night tossing and turning.

Previously, I had worked with law enforcement in several Southern California jurisdictions as a "psychic detective." Most involved missing children or spouses; two were homicides. The next day, I contacted a detective acquaintance to discuss my impressions.

An hour later, he called back. He asked me to drive down and meet with another detective. The boy's disappearance was being treated as a missing person case, but the detective had some questions and wanted to meet face-to-face. I agreed.

Shortly before I reached the boy's town, I drove by a vast field covered with heavy brush that stretched off into the distance. Suddenly, I felt a depression so intense that I pulled off the road and stared out at the field for at least ten minutes to compose myself. An hour later, I was walking through that field with a detective and four uniformed police officers; two carried shovels.

We wandered aimlessly for thirty minutes, tromping through heavy weeds and brush, and then we came to a small clearing with evidence of freshly dug soil. The officers with shovels began digging and soon uncovered a child's body in a shallow grave. I broke down and became physically ill.

Before I drove home that afternoon, I spent an hour with a police sketch artist. Later, I learned that his drawing of the man I had seen in my mind's eye depicted the boy's stepfather. The man was arrested for murder, and the boy's mother was charged as an accessory. Both were convicted and sent to prison.

After that horrible day, I was depressed for weeks. I had recurring nightmares of the child being beaten. I had begun to feel that my second sight was a curse rather than a gift; and other turmoil was going on in my life at the time, which complicated matters further. I needed a break. I finished my current writing project for Irving Wallace, and then I stopped writing altogether. I stopped lecturing and teaching meditation classes. I quit volunteering at the suicide prevention hotline I had helped to set up at the local Free Clinic. I had decided to take a year's hiatus from it all and use that time to recharge and assess my life goals.

During this difficult time, my wife gave birth to a son, David, who would be my only child. We had been having problems in our marriage, and after David was born, she moved out to live with her mother. By fall, I had drifted into a part-time job as a disk jockey at a trendy Southern California dance club. It was a weird, 180-degree departure from my writing and psychic work, but it was a needed diversion. Weeks went by, and the part-time job turned into a full-time job. I told myself that I would pick up where I left off in six months, then a year, then two years. I wasted the next ten years playing dance music and losing myself in the club scene.

I had no way of knowing then that twenty years after searching for a missing child's grave in a deserted field, I would be forced to search one more time, on MySpace, for the killer of my son, David. He was stabbed to death the weekend after Father's Day in a botched attempt to steal a laptop computer from his car.

"Leave the past behind and move forward" is good advice, but sometimes it's beyond a person's capability when faced with extreme circumstances. If you've experienced a terrible loss, you have probably faced that same dilemma. You may have felt weak because you couldn't "get a grip" and follow this sage advice. But if life were truly as easy as following a cliché, saying a prayer, or making a New Year's resolution, everyone alive today would be ecstatically happy.

It is easy to say in hindsight: "I should have done this, that, or another thing." With hindsight, all the pieces of the puzzle snap neatly into place and we can see the big picture. But we don't have that advantage when we are caught up in a tragedy that tears our emotions open or a situation that unexpectedly explodes into a sudden, full-blown crisis.

No parent should ever have to bury a child, and everything in my life changed after that. I had come to forks in the road of life before and understood their meaning; but this one was incomprehensible. I spent the next few years angry, bitter, and depressed. I lost myself in work; I'm still a workaholic. But eventually, my core beliefs in cause and effect, and that everything happens for a reason, rose from the ashes. The spiritual teachings passed on to me by the woman who rescued me from the streets when I was 17, brought me into her family, and loved me like her own son, were still ingrained in my character. Reawakening those beliefs helped me to begin the healing process and sparked a renewed sense of purpose in life.

Today, I can affirm, based on the deep conviction that comes from walking barefoot on burning coals, no matter what cards we are dealt in life, we must recover and go on. We can take a timeout to grieve, and then we need to make a conscious choice: either accept the role of victim and remain a prisoner of the past, or break out of that prison, rekindle our hope, and become the architect of a future that is like a lump of clay, waiting to be shaped by our thoughts and actions.

I have changed and learned some hard lessons. I'd like to say that I have learned every lesson life has thrown at me, and now I will devote my remaining time in this life to good thoughts and deeds. But I'm human, and like all humans, flawed. Nothing in nature is perfect, and no human being is perfect. Trying to live up to that lofty goal of perfection will only lead to frustration and disappointment. Even the most exquisite rose has blemishes, and those small defects set it apart from every other rose, making it wonderfully unique and beautiful.

As you walk your own path through life, you don't have to be perfect. You can make mistakes—even dumb ones. Despite those mistakes and the flaws in your nature, you can still be a loving, compassionate, spiritual being. Hopefully, you will learn from your mistakes and grow to become a better person. Not perfect, but better. And when the day comes that you bid farewell to this tiny blue speck on a remote edge of the Milky Way, if you leave the world a better place than when you came into it, your life will be a success, and your spiritual destiny will be bright.

Now, what about you—do you find yourself drifting back into the past? Do you reminisce about the happy times of childhood, your adventures as a teen, or your first proud accomplishments as a young adult? Do you fondly relive your first Christmas, your first crush, your first car, or first apartment? It's human nature to take pride in your triumphs and cherish the happy moments of your life. In fact, if you are like most people, you may spend a lot of time recalling warm memories that make you smile.

You might dwell on sad memories too: the first time a loved one passed away, the first time a parent reprimanded you. Some people live with memories of childhood abuse and other scars from long ago. Or you might drift into a sad mood remembering a best friend who moved away; your first love affair that ended on the rocks; the first job you lost. It's natural to wonder *What if?* What if you had made different choices? Things might have turned out better; misfortune or failure might have been avoided.

Living in the past can be deceptively comforting. Your memories may be happier than your conditions in the present. The past is familiar and secure. It's always there. It never changes. You can always find and relive the high points of your life when your spirits need the lift. It may be more comforting to lose yourself in the memories of times gone by than to think about what you lack in the present or what you fear in the future.

Living in the past is like an addictive drug. The more time you spend there, the more absorbed in it you become, and the more time you want to spend there. The more you dwell on memories, the more comforting they become—even the negative and unhappy ones. They're just there. Familiar. You don't have to do anything to hold on to them. No one can take them away.

Living in the past is not only addictive but it robs you of the present and undermines your prospects for success and happiness in the future. Imagine that you are doing sixty-five on the freeway. You avert your eyes from the road and gaze into the rear-view mirror to watch the cars behind you. You ignore the road ahead and keep looking behind you. What will happen is predictable—you'll run off the road or crash into someone. At the least, you'll have to pay for repairs to your car and other vehicles you might hit. At worst, you could injure or kill someone or yourself.

When you dwell on the past, you lose your focus on the present. You surrender your claim to it and let it slip away. It evaporates. The future becomes the present, and it continues to evaporate, minute by minute. You forfeit your chance to shape the future to your liking and miss opportunities because you are focused on the past and don't see them. No thinking person would drive down the freeway gazing in their rear-view mirror. So why throw away your future as you travel the road of life because you are looking over your shoulder into the past?

Richard Alpert, a prominent Harvard psychologist from the 1960s, traveled to India and experienced a spiritual awakening while there. He returned to America calling himself Ram Dass, and he became a teacher and writer beloved by millions. One of his books,

Be Here Now, helped to usher in an era of spiritual thinking in the West. The title of the book is a reference to living in the present, being focused in the here and now. When you live in the present, you realize that the past only matters for its role in shaping you into who and what you are today. You live in the moment and make the most of each passing hour of your life. Your eyes remain unwaveringly focused on the future and your spiritual destiny.

As you go through your daily life in the here and now, strive to be forward-looking and mindful of the future. Before you know it, the tomorrow that you worried about yesterday will be today. Learn from the past, live in the present, and aspire for the future. That is the one certain path to sanity, peace of mind, and happiness. If you learn nothing else from reading this book, let this be the one lesson that stays with you.

Lesson 3

Your Blueprint for Change

Never underestimate the life-changing power of cause and effect. This natural law governs every living and inanimate thing in the universe. It is at work producing effects and results that arise from every action we take and our every thought in daily life. It is constant, predictable, powerful, and inescapable. You may not even realize it is at work in your affairs, but it is the response to every action and the reason for every condition that exists in your life.

Think back over your life, consider the choices you've made and the actions you've undertaken in recent years. You will probably recognize many events and conditions that occurred as a direct result of those actions. In some cases, you made the right decisions and took the right steps to achieve an intended result, and it came about as you hoped. The workings of cause and effect make sense in these situations. But what about instances where you made all the right choices and did all the right things, yet you achieved less than expected or ran off the tracks into utter failure? Or you might look around at the world and wonder why one man's acts of kindness are rewarded with misfortune while another commits heinous crimes and seems to walk away unscathed.

The law of cause and effect, or karma, might not always make sense or work quite as we expect. It might even seem random to an observer. It is beyond human comprehension just as other natural laws are at work in the universe that we don't understand or know nothing about. The fact that we don't know about these wonders or don't understand their workings does not mean they don't exist. Karma operates on a timetable that spans decades and lifetimes. The fact that a motorist drives recklessly and breaks the speed limit does not mean he will be ticketed on that day. He might engage in reckless driving on many days, and it might be months or years before he is caught and pulled over. He might never be ticketed; some other far more serious consequence might come from the cause he has set in motion—for instance, a car accident. On a day that he is driving responsibly and obeying the speed limit, he is involved in a collision. He complains to his family: "Why did this happen? I was driving carefully and I was following the speed limit!" Cause and effect, my friend. Toss a stone in the pond, it will create ripples. Every time.

Humans know almost nothing about the universe, except that it is vast, uncharted, and stretches into infinity all around us. A child may not grasp the physics of lightning, but nevertheless, it exists, and it can be a destructive natural force. The fact that we do not fully comprehend the intricate workings of the law of cause and effect, or it does not work as we expect or would like it to work, means only that we don't truly understand the laws of nature or how they affect our lives.

Fortunately, you don't need to understand karma to take charge of your life and put your affairs on a positive track, just as you don't need to understand electricity to switch on your desk lamp. The two most important constants that you need to keep in mind as you traverse the stormy sea of life are: every action you take will cause a reaction; and you are the maker of your future and master of your destiny. Life will call upon you to make decisions and to act, and you will harvest the fruit of your efforts.

Certainly, you'll encounter situations that frustrate you, as well as delays and even occasional failure. Maybe it is a result of unwise choices you've made without realizing it, or an effect of an earlier cause that you set in motion. Perhaps it was the result of an action you thought was inconsequential, but it had a greater import on the outcome of your endeavor. It could have been that your attitude was clouded by self-doubt or negative thinking, which affected the outcome. Many factors may come into play, and the fact is, you may never know what went wrong. In any event, it's in the past, and what's done is done. You move on and try again, making your best effort to ensure that all the actions you take, and all your thoughts and attitudes, favor the success of the endeavor.

Ultimately, though, the outcome of every undertaking will be determined by the choices you make and the energy you put into it. Invest positive energy and you will help ensure positive results. Inject doubt or other negativity into the mix, and you may impact the outcome as surely as throwing dirt into clear water will produce a muddy and undrinkable brew. The choices you make in day-to-day living will become the stones and mortar of the foundation upon which your future will be built.

Through your choices, and your resulting actions, you may inject yourself into the game of life as just a spectator. Or you may place yourself in situations where you are on the receiving end of effects caused by the actions of other people, and then you become a victim. A third option, and a much better one, is to take charge of the game, become the initiator of positive actions that will produce positive reactions, and you will reap the rewards. Choose the road of failure and unhappiness: Your life will be miserable and your prospects for breaking out of suffering and achieving anything better will be bleak. Make choices that bring your fondest hopes and dreams within your reach: Success and happiness will shine brightly in your life. Every day that you wake up, you choose to do one or the other—either consciously or without realizing it. Which path will you set out upon when you wake up tomorrow?

Some people will find it unsettling to learn that they have this degree of control in life. It's easier to believe that life is random, and that opportunities and good fortune drop from the sky by chance. Luck blesses some people for no rhyme or reason, while others are unlucky. When we take this view, it's easy to blame other people or life itself for our difficulties and failures.

It is a bit scary to accept responsibility for our own actions and the consequences of those actions. It requires courage and perseverance to take the wheel and steer your life towards goals so lofty that an average person might believe they are unattainable. It is hard work to plan intelligently and muster positive, constructive thoughts and actions that will move you towards your life goals. It's scary, too, realizing that you could make mistakes. A decision might be faulty; an action might have unintended consequences. When you are the driver, you can blame no one but yourself for mishaps along the way.

The alternative is to let others drive. But when you choose this option, you cannot steer around obstacles that you clearly see in the road ahead. You become the victim of their mishaps. Likewise, you have no say in the destination. You don't know: Will they make the right decisions every time? Will their goals be in sync with yours? Will you be happy embracing their goals and dreams at the expense of your own? As you can see, taking the easy road and letting someone else make decisions that will affect your present and future might seem like the "easy" option, but it isn't, and the consequences can have a negative and lifelong effect on you.

You can and must do more in life than merely be a passenger or a spectator watching other people live their lives. You have your own life to live, your own road to travel, and your own spiritual destiny to fulfill. You can share the journey with others who are on the same path, pursuing similar goals. In fact, connecting with such people should be a goal in your daily life, because they can have a positive, empowering, and reaffirming influence on you. But you must keep their roles in perspective: they are companions, traveling to the same common destination, and not the controllers of your life or destiny.

"Power Tools" That Can Change Your Life

This book discusses practices and beliefs embraced by many different faiths and inspirational belief systems. We will approach this in a non-denominational way that does not favor one dogmatic view over another. Truth is truth, and it is not owned by any particular group of believers. A short list of terms used throughout this book follows. These methods are known by various names but the underlying principles are universal.

Reality Checks: A reality check is a brief story, usually just a few sentences, that brings into focus a simple truth that might slip your mind as you navigate the complexities of your daily life. These anecdotes provide a way to communicate with the subconscious mind and reinforce a course of action that you may need to take to achieve a goal or desired result. In some belief systems, these stories are called "parables."

Affirmations: An affirmation is a phrase that you say once or repeat numerous times to reinforce a positive behavior or attitude. "I can succeed!" is a popular affirmation. "I do not want a cigarette!" is another. It can be spoken out loud or silently in your thoughts. Either way, the purpose is to affirm something over and over so that your subconscious mind will eventually accept it as true and cooperate with your conscious will. Affirmations are one of numerous tools you can use to help you stay sane, positive, and in control of your emotions and moods as you go through the day.

Balancing Techniques: Certain exercises, such as rhythm breathing, can help you to relax and promote feelings of equilibrium and serenity. These methods are commonly used to manage stress, control anger, promote relaxation, lower blood pressure, and stabilize or "balance" the emotions, among other things. The term "balanced" as used here refers to a state of mind in which your emotions are stable; you are in full control of your moods, desires, and emotions; and you are interacting with your environment and the people around you in healthy, harmonious ways. Simple breathing routines are typically used in balancing exercises, but other methods can be effective too; for instance, meditation and visualization routines.

Balancing techniques are easy to use and effective. Just making a conscious effort to relax can have a stabilizing and healthy effect on the body and mind, even when you only have a few minutes of free time and you are not able to relax deeply. Every little bit helps, and every positive action you take will contribute to a positive result. In the next lesson, a simple rhythm breathing exercise that you can practice will be described step by step.

Meditation: In its simplest form, a mental exercise, preceded by relaxation, where the goal is to focus on a positive thought or feeling. Doing so has a calming or healing effect on the body as well as the emotions. In some meditation practices, the goal is first to relax and then sensitize or stimulate the part of the brain responsible for psychic awareness or spiritual insight. Some who meditate seek to achieve nirvana or a state of spiritual enlightenment.

Meditation can be as simple as focusing the mind on an image, the memory of a beautiful sunset, an uplifting poem, a religious or geometric symbol, a prayer, a mantra (a chanted word or phrase), or anything else that provides a focal point and allows the meditator to reach a state of single-mindedness. Some people who practice meditation for its spiritual benefits are able to attain deep inner peace, harmonious attunement to the Universe or oneness with the Supreme Being.

A variety of morning and evening meditations are presented throughout this book. If you are comfortable with simple forms of meditation, you can perform these exercises and quickly discover the benefits. First, you will need to relax as much as you can. Then, focus your mind on the suggested thought or image for a few minutes or longer. Enjoy the relaxed, tranquil feeling that gradually builds and flows through your body and mind.

Visualization: For this type of exercise, you close your eyes and hold an image, a symbol, or a scene steady in your mind's eye as if viewing it on a giant theater screen. The process is similar in some respects to meditation as just described. First, you relax deeply. Then, you use a simple balancing exercise to promote a state of physical and mental equilibrium. When you are fully relaxed, begin the visualization process.

Visualization is used for various reasons that include attaining a deeper state of relaxation and greater balance; stimulating creativity; increasing psychic sensitivity or spiritual awareness; and improving dream recall. Another beneficial use is training the mind to focus and respond in a desired way. This can, for example, help a person in need of self-discipline to overcome a habit such as smoking or to deal with anger management and other issues requiring emotional self-control.

Daily Regimen: A regimen is an action or a series of actions that you perform every day to reinforce a positive attitude or behavior. It can involve a single routine, such as saying a prayer before going to bed; a physical activity, such as an hour of vigorous exercise; or a nightly routine as simple as of relaxing with a good book or enjoying candlelight. The goal is to replace bad habits, stress, or disharmonious feelings with positive thoughts and habits that will dispel negative emotions and promote physical and emotional balance. You can begin a daily regimen at any time, but it must be done faithfully every day to realize the full benefits.

Harmonizing With the Laws of Nature

In our mundane world, laws are written rules meant to ensure that society functions in an orderly manner. On second thought, some laws are meant to protect the special interests of the people who write those laws, but that's a discussion for another day! Universal laws transcend man's written laws. For instance, "Thou shalt not kill" is a universal law embraced in every major religion, and even in societies that do not believe in a supreme deity. Other universal laws, such as the law of gravity, are immutable and affect every molecule in the cosmos.

Natural laws affect us in both conspicuous and subtle ways every moment of our lives. We can accept and learn to harmonize with them or struggle against them and make living a more difficult ordeal than it needs to be. Paddling a canoe upstream is a struggle, and sooner or later, the task will wear you out. Conversely, going with the flow is easy—so easy that sometimes you can just sit back and enjoy the ride.

Great philosophers, writers, and spiritual teachers have described Newton's Third Law of Motion—*Every action produces a reaction*—in a multitude of ways down through the ages. The core teaching, as we have learned earlier in this book, is that your thoughts and actions plant seeds in your spiritual garden, and over time, those seeds will sprout. Here's another way to look at it:

Reality Check

If you plant bitter herbs in your spiritual garden, you can't expect to harvest sweet corn.

You will have less stress in your life, your goals will be easier to accomplish, and major decisions will be easier to make when you realize that, as the Chinese philosopher Confucius once observed: "There are no coincidences in the universe." There are causes and effects; actions and reactions. Centuries ago, this natural law was referenced in Hindu writings as "karma." The Bible likewise tells us "we shall reap what we sow," and so you should "do unto others as you would have them do unto you." Galileo, Copernicus, Newton, Einstein, and other great minds have explained this universal law in various ways, helping us to see the nexus of cause and effect in the world around us.

It may not be easy, and it might be quite painful, but ask yourself: What actions have you taken in your life, and what reactions came about as a result?

All that you have done or tried to do, and all your accomplishments and failures up to this moment, have been a cascade of cause and effect. You might not see the connection in some of your life conditions; it becomes more and more difficult to see the workings of cause and effect over a longer period of years. For now, just try to connect the dots for a few recent events in your life.

While it's true that everything in your life has a cause-and-effect relationship, you should also understand that you probably did not plant every weed growing today in your spiritual garden. Parents and other family, friends, teachers, coworkers, lovers, and other memorable influences in your life probably have planted some of their own seeds. You may have allowed it; or you might not have been aware of it at the time. Either way, when you don't remove those seeds and replace them with your own, they will grow and eventually bear fruit. Most of what you will harvest from them will not bring you happiness, and you could spend a lifetime struggling with the consequences.

Continuing with our spiritual garden metaphor, you can pick up a hoe right now and begin tilling the soil around you. You can pull up and discard unwanted weeds and replace them with roses. The sooner you start, the sooner you will be able to set course for a brighter future aglow with the positive conditions you've cultivated.

Morning Meditation

Age is a quality of mind.
If you have left your dreams behind,
If hope is cold,

If you no longer look ahead,
If your ambitions' fires are dead—
Then you are old.
But if from life you take the best,
If in life you keep the jest,
If love you hold;
No matter how the years go by,
No matter how the birthdays fly—
You are not old.

— *H.S. Firtsch*

Why Being Positive Is Difficult

Being positive and balanced is hard work. It not only takes considerable effort and self-control to get there, but it's easy to slip back into old habits of depression, anger, and other negative thinking. People cling to these behaviors because they're familiar and have become the norm in their lives. You probably know at least a few of these unhappy individuals, or you might be one yourself. They go to sleep at night depressed, wake up depressed, and somehow get through the day, but a dark cloud is always hovering overhead. They lack emotional resolve, and when a burst of anger or depression sets in, they lack the self-control to return to a positive, balanced state. When dramas and crises are not erupting, they worry that one is on the way and wait for new problems to appear.

Those who think and feel this way in daily life are not necessarily negative people. They simply may be caught up in a negative environment. We expect much of ourselves and others in modern society, and many of us are quick to judge. We assume a person can stay positive or regain equilibrium by "manning up" or "getting a grip." But even a person with great optimism and resolve would have trouble staying cheerful if, for example, they lived in a household with an aging, disabled parent, an unemployed husband, a growing stack of bills, and the phone ringing off the hook with debt collectors.

Your situation doesn't even have to be this dire. If you spend time on the Internet or visit news websites, there is plenty of drama and negativity to be found. It's easy to succumb to anxiety and pessimism. The more we are dwell on these thoughts, the stronger and more deeply entrenched they become. Before long, we see evidence everywhere that the world is a sad and hopeless place. This black cloud of despair is always hovering nearby, but whether you step into it requires a conscious choice. You can learn to avoid it, or if you are caught up in negative thinking, you can learn how to break out and free yourself—it's easier than you think!

Reality Check

If you pour a cup of muddy water into a large pool of clear water, it will disperse. Within a minute or two, the muddy water will disperse and the pool will still appear to be clear. But if you pour a cup of clear water into a murky pond, the clear water will be polluted in seconds and you will see no trace of it.

Think about it: a drop or two of positive energy will have little effect if you are immersed in a muddy swap of negativity. This is why, when a person says, "But I meditated and held good thoughts for a few minutes!" nothing much comes of it, and they dismiss positivity as a waste of time. Before you can see meaningful results from positive thinking, you must pull one foot out of the swamp and plant it on solid ground.

Identifying the major stress points in your life is the first step to pulling yourself out of the swamp. Once you have one foot planted on firm ground and can take a breath of fresh air, you can begin the task of cleansing negativity from your environment.

You probably can readily identify the main sources of stress in your day-to-day living. Perhaps it's the usual culprits: money problems, a dead-end job, an unfaithful spouse, an addiction. Obvious stressors are easy to recognize; but to understand *why* these negative conditions have become entrenched in your life, you must do some soul searching. You can't fix something until you know what is broken! So, let's take a few minutes now to identify the major stress points in your life.

Evening Meditation

"There is a place within each of us that is totally connected with the infinite wisdom of the universe. In this place lie all answers to all the questions we will ever ask. Learn to trust your inner self."

— *Louise L. Hay*
Life: Reflections on Your Journey

Healing Exercise

Sit down in a quiet place with two sheets of paper and a pen. Relax. Inhale slowly and deeply; exhale the same way. Repeat this rhythm breathing exercise for five minutes. Feel the tension gradually dissipate from your body. Block the day's worries out of your mind. Tune out noise and other distractions. No music. No news. Just relaxing peace and quiet.

Without dwelling on any particular problem bothering you at the moment, make a list of the stress points you can identify in your life. Remember, stress can be caused by many things: anger, fear, jealousy, resentment, insecurity, addiction, financial woes, and physical illness or pain, among others. You may have just a few or many stressors in your life. Write down all that come to mind.

When you are finished, number your list. Identify the stressor that concerns you the most today and label it #1. Identify the second most vexing stressor and number it accordingly. Do the same for the third and continue until you have numbered all the items on your list.

Now, review your list and ask yourself: "What can I do to fix these problems and lower my stress?" Write the answers of your second paper. Then, put both sheets away and resume your day.

Tomorrow around the same time, sit down in your quiet space with your two pages of notes. Repeat the relaxation step: Breathe slowly, deeply, and feel the tension ebbing from your muscles. Put the day's worries out of your mind. Then, review your list of solutions — think of this list as a blueprint that you can use to change your life. You have identified the major stress points affecting you and listed steps you can take to resolve them. You don't have to do anything today. Just look over the list and remind yourself of the problems and challenges you need to tackle.

Over the next several days, think more about your "life change" blueprint and try to carry out at least one corrective action on your list. Obviously, some stress points will require much more time and effort to fix than others, but taking the first step will get you moving in the right direction. The first step is often the most difficult!

Lesson 4

Relax, Breath, and Start Living

Stress is everywhere! It's almost impossible to avoid in daily life. It permeates every facet of our existence from the moment we awaken until we go to sleep at night. We worry about money, love, health, and family. We worry about the consequences of past actions, present situations, and what might happen in the future. We fret about things we could easily change and things beyond our control. You may spend a lot of time worrying about the future, even though many of these things probably won't ever happen.

If you completed the exercise in the previous lesson, you should now have insights into the major stress points in your life. Some might have been obvious and easy to identify; others may have been harder to pinpoint. How many stressors are on your list? If it contains more than a few, your life may be in turmoil. If your list is short, consider yourself lucky. But even a few stressors can be fertile ground for physical, emotional, or spiritual dis-ease. If you are listening to a beautiful song, but a discordant gong clangs now and then, even though it is infrequent, this sour note will grate on your nerves and spoil the song.

Have you ever complained, "Why do I feel run down and get sick so often?" You may feel tired and drained, even though you've taken steps recently to improve your well-being. Maybe you quit smoking, improved your diet, started taking vitamins, or stopped drinking. Yet, the symptoms of dis-ease persist. People who are under stress at work, and those trapped in unhappy relationships or caught up other negative situations often suffer colds, headaches, depression, fatigue, digestive disorders, and other maladies.

Healthy habits, a stellar diet, and exercise won't make you feel better if your life is in turmoil or your mind is clouded by negative thoughts such as anger, guilt, fear, and self-doubt. Fortunately, you can learn simple ways to cope with stress. Anyone can master these self-healing methods by learning a few quick and easy steps to relax, balance, and find your inner peace. We refer to these methods as *balancing techniques*.

Reality Check

When body and mind are out of synch with nature (discord), the reaction (cause and effect) is dis-ease.

The First Step to Self-Healing

A variety of exercises can be used for balancing. Two of the most popular are simple relaxation and rhythm breathing. Both are easy to learn, you can use them anywhere, and they require only a few minutes of your time. When you face a stressful situation, you can use these methods on the spot, and the results can be dramatic!

Few things in life are certain, but the self-healing power of nature is a constant we can depend on. Even if you use these methods once in a while and you don't relax as fully as you could, they can still work for you. The day you make a conscious decision to relax, take a deep breath, and shift your mind into positive gear, your life will take a gratifying turn for the better.

In the self-help classic *Be Well* (New York: Random House, 1975), Dr. Mike Samuels M.D. and Hal Bennett write: "If you relax for a moment by enjoying a deep yawn or sigh, you will immediately experience subtle changes taking place in your body. Sighing and yawning are activities we all do in our lives without thinking too much about them. But they are also natural tools which change your body physiology. For example, when you are tired, the reflex to yawn is your body's way of revitalizing tired cells."

The authors go on to explain: "If you follow a yawn or sigh by imagining yourself lying down and resting peacefully, your brain sends signals throughout your body to relax. You'll feel your muscles actually begin to relax. Just as your mind can cause your muscles to tense, it can cause the opposite effect. This ability to relax our muscles, though we don't particularly think about it, accomplishes changes at least as important as tension does. Through relaxation, small blood vessels open and carry increased nutrients, hormones, and antibodies to your cells to revitalize them. Relaxing frees your inborn healing abilities to work at their best. In these simple, everyday acts, you can voluntarily initiate changes in your body through your mind."

The nexus between physical, emotional, and spiritual well-being is well documented, not only in metaphysical writings but medical literature. When your body is well, your emotions mirror this state of wellness. When you are in pain, it manifests through feelings of fatigue, depression, lethargy, and other negative conditions. Likewise, your spiritual health is determined by the state of your physical and emotional health.

The first step to feeling better physically and achieving emotional balance is learning to relax your body. You can then tap into a reservoir of natural healing energy within you. Relaxation will help you melt away tension, anxiety, and other negative emotions, restoring your equilibrium. The mental relaxation that follows physical relaxation will put you in touch with your Higher Self where you will always find a wellspring of wisdom and courage.

Relaxation and Balancing Exercise

For seven to ten days, get into the habit of performing a daily regimen that will help you advance in your personal growth and spark a healing transformation in your life. Spend ten minutes a day performing the relaxation step described below. Try to do it at the same time every day so it becomes a healthy habit and second nature. The best time to do this is in the late afternoon or early evening when your day is over and you have time for yourself. Adjust the timing as needed if you have a different work schedule or you are a night owl.

Go to a quiet room where you can be alone and relax. Turn off the TV and other sources of noise. Make the room as quiet as possible. Adjust the temperature for optimal comfort. The room should be cool and pleasant to relax in. If the weather is mild, open a window for fresh air (as long as it is quiet outdoors). Dim the lights.

Sit in a comfortable chair. Close your eyes and relax. Inhale slowly and deeply to the count of 10. Don't count out loud—do it in your mind. Hold for a count of 3. Then, exhale slowly to the count of 10. Hold for a count of 3. Repeat. Establish a pattern of rhythm breathing for a few minutes until you are completely relaxed.

Focus your attention on your right arm. Relax the muscles in that arm. Feel the tension flow out of it. Imagine a soothing wave of healing energy moving down your arm and into your fingertips. You may notice your arm tingles or feels heavy (or light). Don't worry—these sensations just confirm that you are relaxing. When your right arm is relaxed, repeat on your left arm.

Next, relax the muscles in your face. Start with your jaw, then your lips, cheeks, forehead, and scalp. Feel the tension ebbing away. Imagine a gentle healing energy caressing your skin, flowing into every cell. As you relax more, you will experience a sense of inner peace, a feeling that everything in your life will be okay. It will start out as just a vague feeling of peace, and it will grow stronger until you experience a sense of deep tranquility.

As you will discover, this simple yet powerful exercise is more than just a way to relax physically. Relaxing your body is the first step to emotional relaxation, and the deeper you relax, the more aware you will be of these positive sensations.

Enjoy this moment of respite from the day's pressures. Notice how you feel when you are the most relaxed point so you can bring this feeling back at will the next time you are on the job or dealing with family and friends, and you feel frustrated or stressed out.

Imagine how great life would be if you could slip into this peaceful state at any time, even in the midst of a crisis. With patience and practice, you can do just that! This balancing exercise is one step in your journey of personal growth. It will put you on a positive path and renew your enthusiasm for life. With practice, you can learn to reach this place of serenity and stay balanced every day for the rest of your life!

In the coming pages, we will explore other relaxation and balancing methods to help you achieve a self-healing transformation. We will also learn other steps you can take to achieve a state of whole being and spiritual harmony.

Practice relaxation daily. Be patient with yourself. Trust that life can be gratifying and enjoyable. Dare to dream of the life you want to be living a year from now. Dreaming is the first step to achieving!

Lesson 5

The Courage to Change Your Life

One summer, a student in a meditation class I taught at the Learning Tree in Southern California shared a glimpse of her unfortunate childhood with classmates. Her parents had been killed in an auto accident when she was eight years old, and she was raised by a sexually and emotionally abusive uncle. Another student asked how she had been able to cope the adversity in her your life and grow into a happy, well-adjusted human being.

"It takes a lot of courage to leave behind what you've always known and go off into the unknown. It's a scary place," she acknowledged. "You have to decide what you want—that you want a better life, and refuse to accept you will always be miserable. Never doubt yourself. If you believe you can do it and work at it, you'll make it happen."

This insightful answer touched on three fundamental principles at work in our lives. Achieving success and happiness in your own life will depend upon you being able to apply these principles in your own day-to-day existence:

1. It takes courage to leave the familiar behind and move forward into the uncharted waters of the future.

2. You must decide what you want in life. Set goals and pursue them.

3. Never doubt yourself. Believe you can make positive change, put the effort into it, and it will happen.

Many people fear the unknown. They feel anxious or may even panic when they encounter the unfamiliar. It's not uncommon for humans to fear and reject new ideas. We see many examples of this in history: When challenged with new ideas, normally reasonable people react with disbelief and fear. Galileo had his tongue torn out for daring to state that the earth is round, not flat, as scholars believed at the time.

An article published on the Cracked.com website, *Five Famous Scientists Dismissed as Morons in Their Time*, examines the fates of other geniuses who ventured into the unknown and were rewarded with scorn. A few examples:

Gregor Mendel pioneered the science of genetics. His theories changed the world, but scientists of his day couldn't understand what he was saying. So, they ignored him. Sixteen years after his death, they figured out what he was saying, and it was brilliant.

In the 1960s, Russian-American physicist George Zweig discovered evidence confirming the existence of quarks, an elementary particle and fundamental building block of matter. His breakthrough revolutionized the field of physics and set the stage for even greater advances. For his effort, he was publicly ridiculed as a charlatan and blackballed from a major university.

Ludwig Boltzmann, a 19th century scientist, proposed the existence of atoms and later pioneered the study of statistical thermodynamics. His work opened the door to quantum mechanics. His reward for being a genius before his time: He was publicly shamed and committed suicide by hanging himself.

Fear of the unknown is the driving force behind fear of change. Change leads you away from the familiar and into the nebulous realm of the unknown. You don't know where change will lead so you resist it, even when you may know it is necessary and desirable. In fact, change is inevitable. Life itself is a process of change. When you cling to negative thoughts or conditions because they are familiar, you ensure that your future will hold more of the same. Discord breeds more discord, and dis-ease left untreated weakens the body and soul, producing more dis-ease.

By resisting change, you also slam the door on potentially wonderful opportunities. As the saying goes, nothing ventured, nothing gained. Instead of embracing change and welcoming new possibilities into your life, you repeat the same mistakes with the same unhappy outcomes.

The power of "negative affirmation" is very real. It is just as potent as the empowering force of positive affirmation. Here are a few examples of negative affirmations that many people practice:

— I will not change because I fear change.

— I will not improve my life because I don't know how.

— I will not try to heal myself because I am too broken.

— I will not try to make a better life because I don't deserve it.

— My life always has been lousy, and I will always be unhappy.

As you can see, not all affirmations are positive or empowering, and you should not practice these. But you may be doing it unconsciously. Sometimes, we let negative feelings sabotage our endeavors, even as we hope for success and work towards a particular goal. You may have practiced negative affirmations yourself in the past. Think back over recent disappointments and see if you can identify traces of negative thinking that influenced the outcome. You might be surprised by what you find.

Most people don't understand why they succumb to negative thinking. After all, why would anyone want to plot their own failure? But look around at your friends and family, your colleagues at work and your neighbors. You'll see intelligent people working hard every day to sabotage their hopes and dreams.

Because it's such an important point to remember, it bears repeating. People cling to negative feelings and life conditions for the same reason they resist change: these problems are known, familiar, and change could bring new problems even worse than the current ones. This attitude is self-defeating, and it's at the root of most of the discord and unhappiness in our lives.

Human beings possess great ingenuity in the mundane world. We build things. We discover. We have keen insight in science and industry. Yet, many people lack good sense in the way they live our lives. If a fire breaks out in the kitchen, you would not hesitate to put it out. If your car is belching smoke, you would drive to a repair shop to have it fixed. But if your life is broken, you may bury your head in the sand, say a prayer, and hope for the best. Deep down, you know that doing nothing will allow past failures to repeat, yet you do nothing—and the past repeats.

Reality Check

Winter is approaching and the roof on your house is leaking. You decide not to fix it because you are afraid you won't do it right, or you might fall off the roof, or some of the leaks might still drip. So, you do nothing—at least you know where to put the buckets! But as time go by, the roof deteriorates. Finally, it collapses. Your home is flooded and your possessions are destroyed.

People conjure up many creative excuses for avoiding change. Some let change happen on its own. They do nothing to control the outcome and plant no seeds that will bear fruit—they just pray for a miracle. When it doesn't materialize or the changes that do come are not agreeable, they blame the outcome on someone or something else, since they did not act of their own.

Playing the waiting game is a common strategy in life, and it rarely turns out well. You wait for someone to fix a problem, which may take a long time or doesn't happen at all. Finally, you must deal with it yourself, and you have nothing to show for the wait but frustration. You wait for a spouse, parent, boss or friend to come to their senses and see things the way you do, or at least compromise. But they don't. So, you give the person a second, third, and fourth chance; and you keep waiting. But nothing changes or improves.

Christianity teaches: "The Lord helps those who help themselves." To see change in your life, you must initiate it and put forth the effort to help yourself. But before you act, however, you need to root out negative and self-destructive thoughts that could work against your success.

Hoping for a miracle is a recipe for disappointment and failure. Yes, someone always wins the lottery, and it *could* be you—but the odds are several hundred million to one that it won't be you. If you want to see change or improve your situation in life, take meaningful action to turn your hopes and goals into reality.

Avoid procrastination. You cannot finish a task until you start it. You can't move closer to a goal until you take the first step. And once you take that step, if you don't keep moving forward, you will never reach your destination. So, do something definite, even bold, to advance yourself in the game of life. Today is a good day to take that first step.

Never surrender to the false notion that you are a "victim of circumstance" or that life has dealt you another losing hand. If the thought creeps into your mind, flush it out. Consciously reject it the moment you recognize it. If you allow it to remain, it will become a catalyst of self-defeat, undermining your efforts without you realizing that you are the maker of your own misfortune.

Almost everyone falls into negative thinking occasionally, and this likely includes you. You may have anxieties and fears; you might doubt your abilities and whether you are capable of reaching the goals you have set out to achieve. These attitudes were probably formed long ago, and now, feeling pessimistic and expecting failure have become a habit. The good news is: you can break this habit! You can weed out and discard negative attitudes that work against you and replace them with positive attitudes that will help you achieve what you desire.

You have a right to happiness because a spark of divinity shines within you. You are a thinking, feeling human being with a heart and a soul. Don't be afraid to step out of the shadows and let the light within you shine through.

Affirmation

I will embrace change with open arms.

I will leave unhappiness behind.

I will replace self-doubt with positive thoughts that will help me move forward.

I will replace tears with joy, failure with success, and discord with harmony.

I will change my life for the better!

Many things in our physical world are self-evident. For instance, as we discussed earlier, the law of gravity assures us that if you toss an apple into the air, it will come back down. Here are a few more laws of everyday living to keep in mind:

— You cannot win a race if you stand still.

— You cannot succeed if you do not try.

— Life offers no guarantees, but one thing is certain: you won't succeed if you don't pursue the goals that matter to you.

Setbacks and failure serve a purpose: they give us opportunities to learn and explore other paths that could may lead to better outcomes than your present course. Children do not learn to walk without falling. Falls can be painful, but soon the child learns how to avoid them. We are all toddlers learning to walk on the road of life. If you fall, pick yourself and keep going.

Looking for Answers in the Right Places

As you weigh the pros and cons of making life changes and you ponder important decisions, remember: you have a wellspring of knowledge at your fingertips. You were born with it. It exists in your higher mind or spiritual self. Look there and you will find answers to all of life's questions and challenges.

You have an inner voice that speaks to you. Some call it intuition, a sixth sense, the spirit or soul, or the higher mind. You might think of it as God residing within you or whispering to you. Learn to tune in to this inner voice—it is the best advice you will ever get. Listen to it. Act on it. Right now, in your heart and soul, you know what you should be doing in life. You know why you are here and what you must do to fulfill your spiritual destiny. You were born with this knowledge, and your inner voice reveals it.

Once in a while, you might think answers aren't there for you. Or you may face difficult obstacles that you don't know how to overcome. When you walk a spiritual path, help always will be there when you need it. This help or guidance may come to you in various ways—through a chance encounter with someone at work or on the street; in a premonition or burst of insight; through a child's innocent remark; in a dream; or in other ways. Keep your eyes, ears, and mind open. Trust that if you ask the right questions, the answers will always be revealed to you.

A Note on Evaluating Your Stress Points

You might have decided to skip the Stress Inventory exercise in Lesson 1. Some people believe that dwelling on stressors in their lives will give more fuel to those problems. But the opposite is true. Ignoring disharmony breeds more disharmony. If you have a tumor, the last thing you should do is ignore it.

You might not even recognize the major stress points in your daily living. You just react to them and allow them to create discord and dis-ease in your life. By identifying your stressors and writing them down, you take them out of the subconscious and move them into your conscious thoughts. You can then make proactive choices about what will continue to affect you and what you choose to release.

Lesson 6

Visualize the Possibilities

*I*n this lesson, we will explore the benefits of visualization, and I will provide a three-minute exercise to introduce you to this powerful self-healing technique.

Visualization is a form of meditation. It is associated with Tibetan Buddhism, but it has been practiced in many belief systems through the ages. Visualization can take a variety of forms, such as picturing a color or symbol in the mind's eye and holding the image for several minutes. It sounds easy, but visualization requires a surprising degree of practice, patience, and self-discipline. Being able to achieve a state of physical relaxation is a must—so hopefully you have followed the advice given earlier to practice, practice, practice! To find out how important relaxation is to visualization, try this experiment:

Relax and take several slow, deep breaths. Then, close your eyes and visualize a bright, lime-green circle in your mind's eye. Rather than a solid disc, envision a thin, lime-green ring, hollow in the center, against the dark backdrop of the night sky.

Try to hold the visualized image in your mind's eye for three minutes. Don't let other thoughts intrude, and don't allow the circle to change size, shape, or color, even a tiny bit. Discontinue the exercise and open your eyes if the lines waver; if the color brightens, dims, or changes to another color; or if the circle fades or changes to another shape.

You may think, "This sounds easy!" But almost everyone who tries this exercise is surprised to learn that on the first several attempts, they cannot remain focused on this simple image for more than a few seconds. Some can't visualize the circle at all.

If you recall our previous lessons, you might have an idea about the purpose of this exercise and why it is not so easy to perform. When your body is relaxed and your mind undistracted, you can balance emotionally. When you are balanced, it is easier to focus on one thought, whether it's a visualized image, a spiritual focus such as a prayer, or a feeling like a sense of tranquility. This mental state of focused awareness is called "single-mindedness."

Stress, dis-ease, and other negativity in daily living cause emotional imbalance, which disrupts your concentration. The more stressed you are, the harder it is to relax, balance, and focus your thoughts. As your stress grows, you may experience an adrenalin rush—the so-called "fight or flight" response. It is supposed to energize you to deal with imminent danger, but in everyday life, it triggers more fear and stress, making it even harder to relax. It's a classic "catch 22." Problem A causes Problem B, and A + B causes Problem C, pushing you into a destabilized condition before you realize what is happening.

Because your physical and emotional state profoundly affect your ability to balance and focus, a simple visualization exercise like the one described above can be used as a barometer of stress in your daily life. When you are stressed out, you'll find it is more difficult or impossible to perform the exercise. The more balanced you are, the easier it will be to focus and the more successful you will be at visualization.

Daily Regimen

Just as physical relaxation produces a calming effect of well-being, visualization can be a useful tool for attaining a state of balance and inner harmony. Relaxation is a self-healing process that occurs on the physical level. Visualization can be a self-healing process that occurs on the emotional, mental, and spiritual levels. Add the exercise above to your daily regimen. Relax as deeply as you can and then do the exercise.

When you first try visualization, don't worry about how well you are doing, and there's no need to time your sessions. Your results aren't as important as the fact that you practice daily. Moreover, your results will vary from one day to the next. Many factors come into play: your mood, health, surroundings, level of self-discipline, even room temperature. You'll have good days, great days, and some days that don't go as well. Practice every day and your visualization skill will develop naturally.

When body and mind work together harmoniously, balance and tranquility are the norm. Thus, we rise above the chaos and discord of the mundane into the balanced, harmonious, and peaceful state of Whole Being.

Morning Meditation

"Most of the important things in the world have been accomplished by people who have kept on trying when there seemed to be no hope at all."

— *Dale Carnegie*

Words of Wisdom—Coping with Fear

When I taught a course at Virtual University based on these lessons one summer, a student posted an insightful comment on the class discussion board. It was in response to the lesson on *The Courage to Change Your Life*, which is Lesson 5 in this book. I would like to share it with you:

"Courage is the ability to act even when your fears urge you not to act. Fear is the illogical side of your mind, the opposite of logic, and a de-motivator. Try to recognize when you are slipping into the faulty logic of fear. If you find yourself saying *always* or *never*, then you are in a trap of your own making. Nothing in life is that absolute.

"The next time you say *always* or *never*, try to think if there has ever been an exception to that. Then think of a second exception. Write them down. Read through your notes from time to time and you will see that your fears are not as real as you thought. This works for depression, anger, jealousy, and other negative emotions.

"Here's another example: If you find yourself thinking 'I always screw up friendships,' think back to a time when you had a good friend. Write down a few notes about what was wonderful about that friendship. What did you do to make the relationship close or meaningful? What good times did you share? Learn from what you did right instead of obsessing on what you did wrong.

"I was once a shy person. I honestly believed that I was shy. But I forced myself to be outgoing. By acting contrary to what I believed, I learned to handle my shyness. Today, no one believes I am shy except me, and only sometimes!"

Evening Meditation

Learn to see, and then you'll know there is no end to the new worlds of our vision.

— Carlos Castaneda

Lesson 7

Creating Your Own Destiny

Life can be as wonderful as you let it be. The cards you are dealt from day to day don't matter as much as how you play your hand in the game of life. Christopher Reeve was an amazing example of this, proving that no matter how great the adversity, life is what you make it. The handsome actor, who starred in the movie *Superman,* suffered a fall from a horse that left him paralyzed. In that instant, his life changed forever. Most people would have given up; but courageously, and with the love of his devoted wife, Dana, the actor went on with his life. Before he passed away in 2004, he was able to rise above his disability to direct and star in several films, and he appeared before the U.S. Congress as an advocate for millions of physically challenged Americans.

You probably know family and friends who have faced far less difficult challenges and complain that life is not worth living. How many times have you thrown up your own hands in despair when things didn't go as you had hoped? It is all too easy to dwell on negatives and ignore the positives working in your favor that can help you turn your goals and dreams into reality.

Reality Check

Every day when you awaken, you make a conscious decision to be happy or unhappy. When you wake up tomorrow, how will you decide to live the next 24 hours of your life? Will you be negative and expect the worst? Or will you be positive and optimistic, turning obstacles into opportunities and enjoying life to the max? How you answer this question will set the stage for tomorrow and the remaining days of your life.

Writing in *Life! Reflections on Your Journey* (Carlsbad CA: Hay House, 1996), author Louise Hay explains: "This moment is all we have. What we choose to think and believe and say now is forming the experiences of tomorrow, next week, next month, next year. When we focus on our thoughts and beliefs right now in the present moment, choosing these thoughts and beliefs with the same care we might select a gift for a special friend, then we are empowered to set a course of our own choosing in our lives."

Don't let the parade of life pass you by. Live for the moment. As spiritual teacher Ram Dass (introduced earlier) taught:

Be Here Now!

To revisit a point made earlier, this is not an obscure Zen saying. It simply means live in the now and make every day of your life count. You cannot recapture lost moments or change the past. And if you wait until "someday" arrives to make positive changes in your life, you could find that someday has turned into yesterday. If you want to succeed and be happy today, if you want a lifetime of success and happy memories to cherish as you go through the years, the time to start building those memories is now.

Morning Meditation

"The problem is not that there are problems. The problem is expecting otherwise and thinking that having problems is a problem."

— Theodore Rubin

Making a Conscious Decision to Be Happy

Not every day will go the way you'd like, and not every decision you make will produce an optimal result. Life is a learning experience, and we learn as much (or more) from our mistakes as we do from our successes. At times, you may feel depressed and alone with your worries. No one is immune to this. How you cope with the day-to-day ups and downs of your life is what matters, and it's a conscious choice on your part. Will you waste your time and energy making mountains out of molehills? Or will you respond to setbacks and tackle obstacles with gusto, determined to move beyond them to discover and enjoy the good things life has in store for you?

The Morning Meditation on the previous page is worth repeating: "*The problem is not that there are problems. The problem is expecting otherwise and thinking that having problems is a problem.*" When the going gets tough on a difficult day, repeat this affirmation in your mind, or say it out loud. Make a conscious decision to remain optimistic. Know that every challenge you encounter serves a purpose. Resistance forces determined human beings to grow emotionally and spiritually, in spite of themselves!

Writing in *Wisdom of the Mystic Masters* (West Nyack NY: Parker Publishing, 1974), Joseph J. Weed explains: "Even though we accept the fact that man is a free agent with the power of free choice, it is still necessary to consider the nature and source of the impulses, urges, and temptations that come before him and call for him to make a choice. If these diverse opportunities did not present themselves, and if these varying impulses and urges were not occurring each month, there would be no reason for him to have free choice. Nor would he have occasion to reason or to think or to use his will."

Is the Glass Half-Full or Half-Empty?

When you look at a partly filled glass of water, do you think to yourself that it is *half-full* or *half-empty*? Your answer is important because it reflects your outlook on life. If the glass is half-full, this attitude probably has been influencing your thoughts and obstructing your quest for happiness for a long time. Change your perspective, and you will change the direction of your life as well as your destination.

Life will always be a struggle for the pessimist. It is just a matter of when and where difficulty will befall him. The sun will always be setting, night's shadows will always be approaching, disappointment will lurk around every corner. On the other hand, if you are an optimist, life may be a struggle at times, but you will flow with the tide, learn from mistakes, and turn setbacks into opportunities whenever you can. Even in the darkest hours of night, dawn will always be approaching, and the sunrise of each new day will shine the light of hope into your life.

Dr. Michael Samuels discusses the importance of making the conscious decision to change your life in his self-help classic *Be Well* (ibid.):

"The decision to be well is the first step in creating ease rather than dis-ease. It is a conscious mental act. You begin it in the same way you might begin a trip to the mountains. You make plans. Making the decision is the first step, but an extremely important one, in a natural growth process."

Life will give you many opportunities to turn dis-ease into ease and unpleasant conditions into pleasant ones. New Year's resolutions are only as good as your intent to follow them, but when you have the will, they can help you to swap negative habits for healthy ones. They are one more tool you can use to help ensure that the year ahead will be rewarding. Likewise, "spring cleaning" is more than a chore to remove clutter from your attic—it is a time to clean disorganization from your thoughts and your life.

You attract what you are, and what you attract reinforces who and what you are. What you expect in life may very well be fulfilled, at least in one form or another. For pessimists, things always go wrong and will always get worse because that is what they expect. Optimists believe everything will work out—and it always does.

Creating a Road Map for Change

In Lesson 1, I suggested that you make a list of stress points in your life and a second list of positive steps you can take to remove to minimize these sources of frustration and anxiety from your life. Assuming that you have done so and moved your thoughts into a positive sphere. Here is another challenge for you:

Retire to the quiet place where you practice your daily regimen. Have paper and pencil or your laptop handy. Relax. Drift into a peaceful state. Then, make a list of all the positive things in your life. List your skills, talents, and character virtues. List the people and conditions in your life for which you are grateful. Write down everything good about yourself as a person and about your life. Don't forget to list simple things often taken for granted such as good health, vision, the fact that you have a job, a roof over your head, and food to eat. After you have listed everything that comes to mind, resume your day.

For the next forty-eight hours, continue to think about other positives you can add to your list. Keep a notepad or your laptop handy and write them down. Then, merge your notes together and put the list in a safe place where you won't lose it.

You now have an inventory of the positives in your life, and this book has given you a set of tools you can use to chart a path to happiness and success. Sit down with your positive inventory and review it from time to time. Add to it. Try to think of ways you can enhance the positive qualities in your life even more. When you encounter frustration or disappointment, or your affairs slide into disarray, review the list to remind yourself of what is right in your life and that a bright future lies ahead if you choose to pursue it and take the steps necessary to reach it!

Evening Meditation

"Every man has his own courage and is betrayed because he seeks in himself the courage of other persons."

— *Ralph Waldo Emerson*

Enjoy Your New Life!

I hope you have found these short lessons useful and that what you have learned will stay with you in the years to come. Above all, remember that positive thoughts, words and actions are the key to happiness, and your life can be as wonderful as you let it be. As you move forward on your life path to fulfill your spiritual destiny:

> Exemplify the positive in your thoughts and deeds.

> Express your creative potential.

> Use your imagination to turn ordinary life events into extraordinary life experiences.

Share, and you will be richly rewarded.

Teach others, and you will discover your own learning in the school of life has just begun.

Be courageous, and you'll not only succeed, but you will make the world a better place.

Be truthful, generous, and kind, and your light will dispel shadows from the lives of those around you and illuminate the path to your destiny.

Our planet Earth is inhabited by 7.5 billion people. What happens in the world from day to day, and whether it becomes a utopia or a living hell, ultimately will be determined by the actions of individuals. You can change yourself, and by doing so, you will, at least in some small way, change the people around you for better or worse; and they will change others. So, think about it: You can change your life. You can change the lives of those you love. You can change the world. It begins with you and your choice to express positive thoughts, words, and deeds in your everyday life.

In the ancient land of Nepal, people greet one another with the word *Namaste!* (pronounced nuh-MAHS-tay), which means: "I honor the light within you." In her book *Acquainted with the Night* (Taylor, Allegra. London: Ebury Digital, 2012), the author adds further light on its meaning: "I honor that place in you where the Universe resides. And when I am in that place in me and you are in that place in you, there is only one of us."

Until we meet again, approach each day as an adventure, an opportunity to learn, and one step on the glorious road to fulfill your spiritual destiny.

Namaste!

Part II
Share the Light

Lesson 8

Wisdom Is Knowledge Applied

The journey to a life of happiness, and the challenge to remain positive and balanced in everyday living continues in this second part of the book. At the conclusion of my inspirational classes that I teach at Virtual University, I invite my students to share insights they have gained by writing lessons they would want to share with future students. In these next pages are nearly two dozen such lessons written by individuals from all walks of life who applied the principles of positivity to change their lives for the better. I am proud of the students whose lessons and life stories are included here, as well the many others who completed my classes. I'm reminded of the saying: "We are all students, and we are all teachers." As you read these lessons, you will appreciate how true that is!

Living in a Material World

Knowledge is eternal. Even in civilization's darkest hours when war, famine, and disease pushed the planet into chaos, the light of knowledge has endured. The means to restore harmony and dispel the discord and darkness from our world have always been close at hand.

Knowledge transcends materiality. It does not depend on human acceptance to exist or be true. The fact that we do not understand or accept a natural law does not mean it doesn't exist. The law of gravity existed long before Newton tossed an apple into the air and understood why it fell back to earth.

Knowledge is universal. It cannot be owned, trademarked, or bottled. It is not indigenous to any language, race, country, or religion. It is a gift from the universe. It shines light into our lives when it is most needed, coming from sources and in ways we least expect, and in its own time. We can hasten its arrival by taking steps to open our minds so we can receive and comprehend it.

In today's world, we like to think that we are in charge of writing the rules as we develop new technologies and scientific marvels unfold. We believe we are discovering new frontiers, just as Columbus thought he had discovered America. The continent had been discovered long before he visited it; he merely found what others already knew existed. The world as we know it is the center of human existence, but in the big picture, it is a tiny speck among millions of stars, and the history of our civilization is a grain of sand in the hourglass of time.

Knowledge is a dependable constant. Natural laws existed at the beginning of time. They have always been with us and will exist until the end of time. The laws of cause and effect, the physical laws of nature, and universal laws that govern the soul's progression are timeless.

The goal of the writings in these lessons is to give you a glimpse of your higher purpose and help you chart a positive and fulfilling journey through life. Using daily meditations and other tools discussed earlier in this book, you will be able to gain insights into why things happen, and how you can turn obstacles and setbacks in life to your advantage. You will learn how others have be able to stay sane, positive and balanced in a crazy world, and how you too can achieve inner balance in your own life despite the drama and chaos going on in the world around you.

As explained earlier, when a lesson in this section suggests meditation or another exercise, choose a quiet time and place. Set aside fifteen to twenty minutes, preferably in the evening when you have quiet time. Use the deep relaxation and rhythm breathing exercises given earlier to relax and balance before you proceed.

In these lessons, you will find many practical insights, and you'll discover a variety of spiritual tools to help you cope with daily stress and negative conditions. Enjoy these readings, and I hope the experiences of others will inspire you to share the light with your family and friends as you journey through life.

Lesson 9

Make Every Day Count

by Phoenix

It is so easy to dwell on the negatives in our daily lives—the meeting we don't want to attend, the dentist's appointment we've been dreading, the stack of bills that need to be paid. Sometimes it is difficult to appreciate or even remember the positive things in life. But it doesn't have to be that way! It's easy to approach daily chores with a positive attitude, and it is much more rewarding.

Negative thinking is a learned behavior. We succumb to it in part because we accept it as normal and expect it in our lives. Some or maybe all of our family and friends have been victims of negativity and pessimism for as long as we can remember. It is reinforced by sad images of violence and tragedy every time we browse news on the Web or turn on the TV. Because it's always there, and it's a habit, we let negativity color our thoughts and control our lives.

We invent humorous and trite sayings to justify negative thinking. For instance: *If something can go wrong, it probably will! Cheer up, things could be worse! Don't wish for something, you might get it!* We joke about it and allow it to influence our affairs, and then we wonder why we wake up angry, frustrated, or depressed. We've been exposed to it for so long we have lost touch with the positive. We've forgotten how to be happy and optimistic. We no longer believe life will always work out for the best, and we expect the worst.

Today is a good day to stop and think for a few minutes about what is good and right in your life. Recall happy times you have enjoyed recently, and remember how it felt in those moments to be positive and optimistic. Remember how to let light shine into your life, and let it happen. Get in touch with what makes you optimistic, what makes you smile, what makes you feel life is worthwhile. Identify those catalysts, and begin adding them back into your life. If they are already there, focus on them in the here and now. Remember, positive thought leads to positive action, and through those actions, you can change your life for the better.

Life is a gift to be savored. Too often, we let life pass by and miss so much. How often have you heard someone say that the year just flew by? Where did it go? Twelve months evaporated! We lose the present when we dwell on the past (which can't be changed) or fret about the future (which doesn't exist yet, and when it does, it will be the culmination of what you are doing in the present). Live in the present moment. Appreciate, enjoy, and learn from every experience as your life unfolds. Rather than dwelling on how many hours you have left to work before you can go home from your job, put that energy to good use and accomplish worthwhile tasks. Instead of stewing that your job is a dead-end, be grateful you have a job when so many people do not. If you don't like your job, instead of fixating on what you dislike about it, take action and lay the groundwork to find one you like better.

Many of us face day-to-day struggles raising kids. Yet, these challenging times will also be the source of our fondest memories when our children are grown and we look back over the years. Don't get so caught up in day-to-day routine that you can't relish good times and laughter in the here and now. Sooner than you think, your kids will be grown and out the door. You will never be able to recapture the innocence of youth or make up for missed hugs and special occasions you were too busy to attend.

I have gained so much from this course. In thinking back over my life, I have regrets, but I know that I cannot change the past. However, I can learn from the past and not repeat the same mistakes. I can look for the positive in each day and make every remaining day of my life count. I see this change in philosophy working in my life already. Every day is a new experience, and I am creating wonderful tomorrows by my actions today.

Make today the first day of a wonderful new life. Take just five minutes, relax, turn off your worries, and meditate on how you would like the rest of the day to go. Practice rhythm breathing.

Inhale slowly through the nostrils, exhale slowly through the mouth. Clear the mind of worry and distractions. Enjoy the relaxed feeling and sense of peace as you focus on the positive experiences you'll attract or create in the days ahead.

Practice this exercise daily or morning and night to bring positive energy and light into your thoughts. You can't avoid occasional thorns in your rose garden, but you can control how you react when you brush against one.

In the morning, meditate on the day to come. Visualize what you want to happen. Focus on your goals and put positive energy into them. Banish doubt and negative thinking from your mind. In the evening, relax and meditate on the good moments during the day, no matter how trivial they might be. Relive the laughter, the clump of flowers you noticed in bloom, the bright smile of a friend (perhaps in response to your own!), the peaceful, drifting clouds in the sky overhead.

Enjoy life one day at a time. Celebrate the present moment. Wake up, smell the roses, and have a beautiful day.

Lesson 10

Seeking the Spiritual

by Vanda

What is truth? Why do some people receive guidance so easily from the Universe, while others struggle with the simple chores of daily living? Why do the same actions, taken by different people, lead to different outcomes? These questions have perplexed human beings since the dawn of civilization.

Almost everyone today is searching for happiness. But because happiness can mean different things to different people, it is an elusive concept. It can take the form of financial success, romantic gratification, good health, friendship, indulging a creative endeavor, or many others things. We pursue it in life like a moving target; it's hard to catch, and more elusive to hold. But it is an attainable goal, and one within your reach right now. Your Higher Mind knows your personal definition of happiness, and it knows how and where to find it. Your inner voice will tell you what it is and how to get there.

What's important to realize as you pursue happiness is that, whatever it means to you and wherever you find it, all roads in life lead to the same destination. Happiness derived from material and sensory gratification is an illusion. It is temporary, fades away, and will always leave you wanting more. Eventually, you will feel deep down that your life is missing something, and your search for happiness will turn to seeking the spiritual. The following insights may guide you on the first steps of that journey.

Self: Timeless and Ageless

Spiritual is an intriguing word. It has the power to make people argumentative and uncomfortable. It is a word used often today. It calls out to us from bookstore shelves, and thousands of websites are devoted to discussing its meanings and practice. My dictionary definition of *spirit* is: "the immaterial part of man; the soul..." In metaphysical teachings, the spirit is one of four levels or aspects of human existence: physical, emotional, mental (or intellectual), and spiritual. These levels correspond to body, heart, mind, and spirit (or soul). Each of the four is progressively finer and less tangible, but they all work together to shape and sustain a living, conscious being—you.

Recognizing and honoring your spirit as the essence of who you are means you don't think of the spirit as being outside yourself or something tenuously attached that you have to search for. Your spirit is your true self. It does not age. The wrinkles you see in the mirror aren't you. The body grows old, the mind grows forgetful, and the emotions grow weary, but the spirit never tires and never forgets.

Another name for your spirit is your Higher Self. We say "Higher" because it is the blueprint, the template, for who you really are. Consequently, it is important for you to recognize the design and follow the pattern.

Some of us are so caught up in day-to-day events that we have forgotten who we are. We have lost touch with our Higher Self and lost sight of our spiritual destiny. Those who recognize only the physical world and do not believe in the existence of the soul see human beings as a cosmic accident. They view our lives as random and without purpose. But metaphysical thinkers believe we are here for a reason, and our ultimate destiny is to liberate our souls from the trappings and bonds of the temporal world.

A wonderful "knowing" settles in when you embark on the search for your spirituality. Tools exist that you can use to help you in this journey, and some are discussed in the next pages. I will also share some of my own experiences along the way. Our life paths may be similar and our destination is the same, but your journey is uniquely yours.

As you begin seeking the spiritual, you should keep a journal. It can be a bound leather book, a simple notebook, or notes on your laptop or desktop computer. This is a first step in acknowledging that you have recognized YOU at last. Through this small act of attention, of writing things down and keeping a record, you will discover that your Higher Self does talk to you. By writing down what it reveals, you affirm that you value the insights imparted to you. You are opening the door to Intuitive Knowledge and expanding your awareness of who you are and the universe around you.

Coming to know yourself and discovering your true nature as a spiritual being requires many steps, but it has significant rewards. It is a process of balancing and self-healing. Thus, you balance and heal your body, emotions, mind, and soul as part of the process. You'll develop talents you might never have seen in yourself. You also may discover your Higher Self has a great sense of humor. I'll share an example with you:

I was going through a transitional stage in life, leaving behind an exciting and eventful period, and entering a more tranquil but somewhat repressed phase of life. I wasn't enjoying it all that much. In fact, I had slipped into an apathetic state. Instead of being creative and motivated, I was watching daytime TV and wasting a lot of time. I knew that I should do something about it, but weeks went by, and I was stuck in a rut.

One morning, I was out walking and marveled at what a beautiful day it was. I heard (or rather felt) a voice within me say, "I need to watch less television." A part of me agreed, but I doubted that I had the will to make that commitment. When I got home, I went straight to the TV to catch the morning news, something I enjoyed. My set is old—it doesn't even have a remote control, but the picture is fine. I pushed the *On* switch, and it popped back out. *On...off. On...off. On...off.* It occurred to me that I was getting a message and I laughed—but I was determined to watch the news! So I held the switch in with a piece of masking tape, and when I wanted to turn off the TV, I removed the tape. I stubbornly watched the morning news every day, but my focus began to drift to other things. I started to paint again. I began to reorganize my life and take control.

Some months later, I was on vacation a thousand miles away, taking another morning walk. I thought to myself, *I know I am over that time-wasting now—I have regained my strength of will.* Mentally,

I tossed the roll of tape in the trash. When I returned home from vacation, I did just that. Since that day, my TV has worked perfectly. I had gotten the message, but more importantly, I acted on it!

You will get lots of messages from your Higher Self if you practice listening for them. Some may come as dreams, and you will have your own language of dream symbolism to learn. Don't waste money on dream interpretation books—your dreams speak to you in your own unique language. We will explore this later, but for now, let's return to the question of seeking spirituality.

What Is Spirituality?

Spirituality is not religion. Religion is a system of beliefs. Being religious and being spiritual are not synonymous. You can be a religious person without being spiritual, and you can be a spiritual person without subscribing to a specific set of religious beliefs. You can be both—religious and spiritual. Or you can have the great misfortune of being neither.

When you decide to embark on a quest to become more spiritually aware, it's like finding a good search engine query on the Web. You do a search and all sorts of exciting possibilities open up. You'll discover there are more options for spiritual growth and more paths to spirituality than you ever dreamed. With so much information and so many choices, the question becomes, which path is the right one? Whose advice should you seek or follow? Which book should you read?

As I mentioned, humans are physical, emotional, mental, and spiritual beings. We are not any one of these exclusively—we are a blend of all four. Each of us is unique, and our paths lead to the same destination, but we are traveling different routes at different speeds. There is no "one size fits all" brand of spirituality, no *right* or *wrong* answers, and no line in the sand telling us what we should and should not do.

Never accept the teachings of any person, book, or religion that states a part of you is unworthy. Your actions and words can be unworthy; your thoughts can be unworthy, but your soul is a spark of the Divine Consciousness, and it is worthy. If you cup your hands in the ocean and withdraw a handful of water, the water you hold is still ocean. You can experience the ocean, touch it with your hands, and enjoy it with your senses, but you cannot limit or contain it. Likewise, your spirit encompasses all. It is one drop in the ocean of the Universe, which is boundless.

What is it that you want or need in life? What are looking for? Perhaps your answer is, "I want to be more spiritual." That answer won't help you achieve spiritual awareness. The goal is too vague and lacks direction. We need specific goals to motivate and inspire us. So, before you can start the journey, you must consider and answer this question for yourself: "What do I truly want?"

Take all the time you need to consider this question. It is so important. The answer may not pop into your thoughts immediately, and you might discard several answers before you find the one that feels right for you. Until you have that answer, you won't know what spiritual path you should walk.

Getting Acquainted With Your Higher Self

Your Higher Self is the essence of your spirit or soul. It contains a spiritual blueprint of who you are. Getting in touch with your Higher Self can give you insights into your purpose in life, your natural born talents, and how to unlock your potential. The Higher Self is the architect of your destiny, but you must do the work necessary to become the captain of your ship.

When seeking to explore your Higher Self, you can gain insights and guidance in many ways. One of the most popular is to use meditation. We can seek our spiritual nature in other ways too. We might take a course on spirituality, listen to music, take a hike in the country, or attend an uplifting event. Discovering the Higher Self will often require stepping away from existing conditions, dispelling negative thought forms, and overcoming self-destructive habits that prevent spiritual growth. Breaking free of the old and embracing the new is a great way to open the door to both emotional and spiritual growth.

In my own life, many of the spiritual answers I have received came through the written word. One day, I walked into a bookstore. I was looking for a book that would give me some direction, but I did not have the slightest idea what book I needed. As I walked up one aisle, a few paces in front of me, a book toppled off the shelf and dropped at my feet. It was a startling experience. It turned out that book changed my life. You might have received spiritual guidance in various other ways. Make it a point to be aware, to tune in, and you will find the answers you are seeking at every turn. I can't tell you how and where you will find your answers, but they will come when you seek them. The Bible tells us, *Seek and you shall find, knock and it shall be answered unto you.*

The book falling at my feet was a life-changing experience for me. Was I praying about my worries in the usual sense? No, I was too full of worry and too caught up in my predicament. But worry can be a form of meditation. I thought nothing could help solve my problems back then. I also wanted an instant fix, a quick miracle. The book falling at just the right moment was my first miracle, but fixing things took time. You may read about people experiencing instant enlightenment, and I know it occurs. It just didn't happen to me that way. I had worked my way into a hole and had to pull myself out of it. It took time to get back in touch with my Higher Self and move forward with my life. I'm still working on it and still on a lifelong quest to develop my spiritual awareness to the fullest.

Why Seek the Spiritual?

Why seek the spiritual? For almost everyone, the answer is: "Because I feel the need," or "Something is missing in my life." You don't know what is missing, but you feel incomplete. Material possessions and sensory gratification are transient—here today, gone tomorrow. The soul is eternal and lives on beyond this mundane world.

When we seek the spiritual, we begin to think in positive ways. We might feel like we are rebuilding ourselves, a little at a time. When you build a house, you know what tools to use and what tasks they perform. Over time and with practice, you'll become skilled at using them. But what tools can you use to explore and develop your soul, and where can you find them?

Life experience itself is the most powerful tool in your spiritual toolbox. Living is a lifelong lesson, and your Higher Self is the teacher. It is all-knowing and eternal. It is the source of your inner voice. If you don't hear your inner voice when it speaks, you are not listening, or you are not understanding the message. Some messages are symbolic rather than direct. My finding a book led to a flood of other books over time. Whenever I asked a question, I found the answer in another book. I was comfortable with that because I love reading. But eventually, I progressed on to other ways of listening.

My search for the spiritual lead me into many interesting life experiences. I joined a local spiritual church, which satisfied my curiosity about psychic abilities such as telepathy, clairvoyance, and astral travel. I read voraciously on these subjects, and I had many wonderful experiences. As my intuition grew, I listened closer. I knew these pursuits were only rungs on my ladder and could hold me back if I lingered on them. I began passing on what I could, teaching courses on relaxation and meditation. I studied Reiki and psychic healing, and I applied them to my own life.

I was learning and growing, yet I felt that I was not learning fast enough. I had been told we learn at our own pace, but patience was a lesson I was slow to learn. I looked for teachers, only to realize those who bounced from one practice to another didn't seem to be learning much at all.

Perhaps you have heard the saying, *When the student is ready, the teacher appears.* I took that too literally. I had hoped one day a knock at the door would come, and a mysterious stranger would be standing there. I would invite him in and he would say he had found me through the dazzling brightness of my aura, and he knew I was ready to learn all the secrets of life. Alas, no such luck. Eventually, I learned that we must work at what we study—there are no free rides.

A Helping Hand From the Universe

I believe I have a guide or guides and a guardian angel. I believe they have helped me in the past and will do so in the future. I don't believe I should expect them to make all my choices for me. Their role is to guide me, not decide for me. Decisions are a conscious process. If we were meant to abdicate decisions, we would not be entitled to claim our life as our own.

One important lesson to learn is that we must always be able to change and let go. This can be hard when, at each step along the way, we feel so sure we have found what is right for us...when we have built something that we think is worthwhile, but now we must detach from it and move on to the next lesson. I don't mean just on a physical level. As our consciousness grows, it keeps integrating knowledge and wisdom that we previously could not comprehend. You may feel a real sense of loss about letting go of old beliefs. It isn't easy, but it must be done.

Where should you start? *Here* is always the right place, and *now* is always the right time. Here in the present, right where you are, is where you will learn your life lessons. You don't need to fly off to a remote mountain to join an ashram or find a guru. You don't need to wear a white robe, although wearing certain colors and eating certain foods may be beneficial. In my case, not eating meat raises my spiritual vibration. You must do what is right for you, and know that what is right for you today might change tomorrow.

If healing calls you, learn about it. Meditation and yoga are wonderful tools. Learn more about them through books or local classes. Do crystals fascinate you? They are beautiful and powerful. Our first radio sets contained crystals. Perhaps they are calling you too. We grow spiritually whether we seek growth or not, and whether the lessons are positive or negative. Growth happens faster the more we seek it.

Investigate all options and seek the ultimate good for yourself and others. Some practices are judged by society to be wrong because of superstition or ignorance. Society is ruled by a group consciousness, and a spiritual pilgrim breaks away from this as their personal awareness grows and transcends the mundane. If you feel confident a certain path is positive and constructive, and it will not harm others, meditate on it. Try it. Pursue it.

What Does Success Mean to Me?

My dictionary defines success as "a favorable result; a hoped-for ending; good fortune. Also, gaining of wealth, position, or other advantage." Most of us desire success for ourselves and the people we love. We may associate success with gaining money, prestige, and power. None of these things are evil, and the adage that money is the root of all evil isn't true. *Love of money* is at the root of evil.

Do you have your sights set on accumulating both material and spiritual wealth? Many books counsel that you can pursue spiritual attainment and prosperity at the same time. Is that really possible? Perhaps. Money is handy to have and being short of it can cause hardship; but obsession with wealth can have negative consequences on our physical, emotional, and spiritual wellbeing.

Before you embark on a spiritual quest, ask yourself what you hope the outcome will be. Will you become a better person by studying insightful materials? Is inner growth your aim? Are you looking for a way to help or heal yourself, your family, or friends? Is it a career move to help you generate wealth and power? Many who have embarked on a spiritual path for the wrong reasons have found that the consequences of exploiting spiritual gifts can be dire.

The quest for wealth and material comfort is not a spiritual endeavor, but there is nothing wrong in wanting to live comfortably. It may even be the catalyst that leads you to seek your Higher Self. That is what happened with me. I was born in a small town, and my parents were not well off, but they managed to provide me an education. I was raised Catholic, and I was seven when my only brother was born. By then, I was already a loner and a voracious reader. I always carried a book with me the way teenagers today carry smartphones.

Two years after my brother was born, I began dropping off to sleep with an imaginary playmate named Danny. He was short and stocky with black, curly hair and a he owned a Border Collie dog. We played together, climbed trees, and went for long walks. We always ended up having a fight and splitting up just as I fell asleep.

One day, I met Danny in real life. I was twenty-one, and after dating for a year, I married him. Interestingly, when he was a child, he had owned a Border Collie. Sadly, we fought often during our marriage and split up several times. After nine years, we divorced. I moved out with our four children and their own Border Collie.

Raising my children as a single mom was difficult, but we survived and they are now happy, well-adjusted adults with their own families. I started a business, enjoyed a comfortable life, and yet I still felt a deep sense of loneliness, despite meeting a good man who helped with my kids' upbringing.

One afternoon, my eldest son dragged me off to hear someone "talk about flying saucers." We were the only people in the audience, and it wasn't flying saucers she spoke of but reincarnation. I was skeptical. I felt there was no proof; but I was curious. The woman we met introduced me to a study group through which I learned about and experienced clairvoyance, auras, psychometry, and other paranormal abilities. Before long, I was hooked! People were just becoming interested in New Age topics; it was new and controversial. Few books on the subject were available at my local library.

I only stayed in this group a few months but long enough to realize there was convincing evidence some people had experiences science could not explain. I also met others who had childhood experiences like mine.

Not long after this, I moved to the city and joined another group that offered psychic development courses. This group was sponsored by the Spiritual Church, where I met many wonderful people who embraced the idea that humans are spiritual beings. The Lord's Prayer was recited every Sunday night, and I loved the hymns we sang. From the podium, visiting psychics gave public readings for the congregation. Apart from donating a little silver to the plate, everything was free, including the healings offered after the service.

After moving to the city, I had two spontaneous astral travel experiences. One was dream-like: I found myself "visiting" my daughter and new grandson in America, two weeks before I actually did. The second occurred in the early morning hours. I was wide awake but sitting in meditation. Suddenly, I saw a velvety darkness, and I was floating in space. A bright light flashed directly ahead. I controlled my excitement and remained focused, aware that I was astral traveling. In apparent slow motion, the light burst into a bright flash and then faded away. Curling tendrils of light spread outwards as I watched and wondered at what I saw.

This experience lasted several minutes. I had no clue what it meant until I turned on the television later that evening and realized I had seen the explosion of the Challenger shuttle as it happened.

Some believe psychic abilities are vestiges of survival instincts early humans possessed to cope with dangers on a primitive planet. Others say everyone has these abilities in some measure, and they are part of a natural sixth sense. Whatever the reality, these gifts must be treated with respect, and they can have consequences when misused.

First Steps to Inner Growth

You are probably wondering how I expect you to learn from what I've written when I have given so few exercises or instructions on what you should do. In fact, it is up to your Higher Self to lead you. I can teach by example, sharing how I studied and how I learned. I can teach you how to paint, but I can't teach you how to BE, because you and your life are unique to YOU!

When you seek the spiritual, you are in a process of growing up. To continue this growth, you read, study, and learn from experience and observation. As you grow, you leave behind the need to rely on others. You think for yourself, interpret your own thoughts, seek your own truths. My goal is to help you learn to think for yourself. The mantra you need is: *I AM*.

As I embarked upon my spiritual journey years ago, I had to learn what part of myself was missing, what healing I needed, and how to go about it. A good student asks questions to find answers, but it may be difficult to find the right questions. A good starting point is to ask yourself, "What do I want?"

Our mission in this life is to awaken as many of our gifts as we can. But our gifts may also be a message, a pointer, towards our true selves. What are your interests? What hobbies do you love? Do you withdraw into yourself when you are occupied with them? Your hobbies and interests may paint an intriguing picture of who you are and give you a message about yourself.

As you continue seeking the spiritual in the weeks and months ahead, stay alert to the whispered guidance from your Higher Self. Live fully in the NOW. Have the courage to be yourself, to seek your Truth, and to live by it. May your life be filled with joys and wonders, and may you greet and end each day with love and laughter.

Lesson 11

A Fork in the Road

by Just a Student

In the early 1960s, no one ever talked about breast cancer, and the media ignored it for the most part. One day, I discovered a small lump in one breast. A week later, a doctor told me it was a cyst and ninety-nine percent of all cysts are benign. He still wanted to remove it so he could verify it was harmless. With the odds ninety-nine to one, I had nothing to fear, just a tiny scar that would not be seen by the world.

When I awoke from surgery with intense pain in my breast area and a metal cage over my chest to keep the blankets away from me, I knew I was the one percent. It was the middle of the night, on a cold, blustery January evening, and I was alone with my thoughts. I had cancer. I was going to die. I didn't want to die. I was in my early thirties. I had a wonderful husband who was always uncomfortable around people with physical ailments, and I had three very young sons.

I started mentally talking to God (a normal reaction for cancer patients). I kept asking why He let this happen. I told Him I was a good wife and mother; I took my children to church and Sunday school. I did a lot of volunteer work to help people in need. Why me? What had I done wrong? The thought popped into my head, "It's what you haven't done..." But I'm getting ahead of myself.

I was deeply depressed. What would I do for my remaining days? It seemed I had two choices. If I took the left fork in the road, I could go on feeling sorry for myself, being depressed, irritable, and this would be how my family and friends would remember me when I was gone. Or, I could take the right fork, put a smile on my face (no matter how bad I felt), and leave my family and friends with happy memories. I chose the right fork. It wasn't easy by any means, but the rewards were great, and each day it got easier. The next morning, I cracked a boiled egg in my hand and yoke ran all over my hand, gown, bed, and floor. I burst out laughing. I knew I was on the right track.

My husband is a rare jewel. He has always made me feel like I am still the sexiest woman on earth. I had decided no woman would take my place with my family after I died so I busied myself teaching my sons how to clean, wash clothes, and cook. My daughters-in-law thank me all the time!

Sometimes I would wonder about "what I hadn't done" that popped into my head the night after my surgery. I wondered how I could find out. After three years of healing, my husband was transferred to a new state, away from my beloved family and friends. Just to keep busy, I joined the volunteers at our local hospital. After a year, my boss found out I'd had a mastectomy and asked me to design a visitation program for the hospital. I did, the doctors approved it, and we set it in motion. The local cancer society also asked to sponsor me, requested my visitations, and supplied me with needed materials. This was a very difficult job as each visit brought back the mental pain and suffering of my earlier days. But the program was a success and is still going today.

At the age of thirty-nine, I was persuaded to go back to college to study nursing. What a tremendous joy this was. I loved every minute of it. But in the middle of my senior year, I became ill and dropped out for a quarter. While I was recuperating, I got a call offering me a position as the executive director of the local Cancer Society. I pondered this, knowing I could use my education and be effective. I decided to take the job and not finish my schooling. My knowledge was more important than a degree, so I accepted the position. The pay was awful, but I didn't need the money. My husband was a great provider.

At last, what I hadn't done was being done. The programs I set up are still in use today, benefiting homebound cancer patients and their families and friends. Hospice is now involved, but that came after I left.

After four years, I was asked to teach in a local college. This had been my goal (teaching) from the start. I taught for eight years. What a thrill it was. It was my reward. Nurses I have taught always thank me, and I'm glad I could teach them.

I felt like I was never really living before I had breast cancer. Life was happy but superficial: I believed clothes and material things were important. Now I know better. Happiness comes from within, and only I can decide to be happy.

As you can see, I am still around—I survived the cancer. I am still married to the same man (forty-seven years). I have watched my sons grow up and watched my grandchildren grow. I have known more joy in the last thirty years than all the years of my life before.

It is said that when a door closes, God always opens a window for you. In my case, He gave me a sun room with lots of open windows. I never stop searching for what I could do to make life better for someone else, and the rewards have been tenfold.

I hope you never come to a fork in the road, but life is full of them. Always remember, happiness is not found in material things. Happiness comes from within and only you can make it happen. Choose the right fork and LIVE.

Lesson 12

Finding Your Strength Within

by Ingrid

Often, we fall into the trap of thinking we are too tired or too broken to make the effort to change our lives. We just don't have the strength or will to strive for a more positive state of being. We don't reach out to seize the happiness and success we desire. Instead, we remain in a state of disharmony and discontent, allowing our negative traits to grow and self-destructive habits to go unchecked. Since that course of action consumes all of our time and energy, we don't cultivate and express talents and positive qualities that we possess.

A good analogy is to compare your life to seashells on the beach. Beachcombers spend hours searching for the "perfect" shell—one shaped just right, brightly colored, and just the right size. The broken shells, the smaller shells, and the plain-looking ones are left behind. Many people identify with the broken and dull-colored shells. They envy the "perfect" people who shine, make lots of money, and bask in fame and popularity. They resent the fortunate people who have an easy life. They don't bother trying to climb the ladder to success and happiness because they have given up or don't believe they can do it with the limited abilities they possess.

Stop for a moment and think about those unwanted, broken shells. On the surface, they seem to have no value, and no one wants them. But they are the survivors. While their cousins sit idly on a bookshelf or are tossed into a drawer and forgotten, the plain shells have weathered countless storms and remain exposed to the elements, yet they endure. They are strong, capable, and unique in their own way.

Carol Hamblet Adams writes in *My Beautiful Broken Shell:* "Broken shells are shells that have been tested...and tried...and hurt...yet they don't quit. They continue to be."

We can learn from these shells. If they can endure the pounding waves and the elements for years or even centuries, then intelligent, resourceful, versatile human beings like you and I can survive the turbulent and painful moments in our lives.

Humans have a strong will to survive, great ingenuity, and a vast reservoir of inner strength. This boundless enthusiasm for life has carried us through the ages, through wars, plagues, and myriad hardships. Our life experiences, including the obstacles and setbacks we encounter, help to shape us and make each of us unique. Our experiences help us to develop the skills not only to survive but to succeed and prosper.

Adams explains: "Broken shells teach us not to look at our imperfections, but to look at the beauty—the great beauty—of what is still left." So, if we look to our inner beauty rather than the illusion of outward appearances, we will find our unique abilities and talents that will help us through life's difficult moments.

I recommend carrying a small seashell in your pocket—one that is unique, broken, or a little flawed. Whenever you have moments of self-doubt or fall into negative thinking, think about or touch that shell and consider all the ways that you too are unique and special. Think of the strengths and talents you possess that can carry you through the occasional storms of your life and on to the many bright, sunny days that await you.

Lesson 13

Acts of Kindness in Daily Life

by Jacqui

I noticed this saying on a bumper sticker and it stayed with me: *Practice acts of kindness and timeless beauty.* I try to live up to this lofty ideal every day. I don't always get the opportunity, but even a friendly smile goes a long way to give a boost to someone who is feeling down.

Acts of kindness don't cost us anything. Dropping in to say hello to an aging relative; being polite to a wrong number phone caller; flashing a sympathetic smile in passing to someone who is having a bad day—these actions require little effort but can bring light into someone's life when they need it. By giving light to others, we strengthen the light within ourselves.

Daily living creates so much anxiety and stress. Sometimes it may seem daunting or impossible to rise above the quagmire. I use several visualizations that I find helpful, and they work well. One method I call the *cloud-tree visualization* is much like the visualization methods taught in this class. I would like to share it with you.

When I am feeling down, I imagine I am a fluffy white cloud drifting across the sky. I hold this thought and tune out all distractions. After a few minutes, I can feel my stress dissolving.

A second, similar visualization method works for me when I am feeling low on confidence. I imagine that I am a tree with a strong trunk and a vast root system spreading through the earth. I focus on how strong and stable I am because of the roots securing my place in the universe. Soon I'm able to feel just how strong and stable I really am.

I use both visualizations often, and still, I am always surprised at how easy and well they work for me. The more you practice these methods, the easier it becomes. The next time you are feeling down or unsure, give these visualizations a try, and the results might surprise you!

> *Beauty surrounds us if we open our hearts and eyes to it.*

Make time every day to go outdoors. Find a serene place in your garden or a local park—anywhere nature abounds. Sit down and relax. Study the trees, plants, and flowers around you. Pretend it is the first time you've seen them, and study them. Look at how the flower petals are formed. Pause to appreciate the colors and textures of the tree bark and leaves, and how the light plays on them. Focus on the colors, the textures, and let these images permeate your mind. You will start to appreciate all the beauty we take for granted so often in our lives.

Every day I am amazed at the wonderful things we have in our world. I no longer take any of it for granted. Life is too short to try and function with our minds cluttered and bogged down in stress. Open your eyes to the beauty around you, and open your heart to the joy of life.

I say, *carpe diem!* Seize the day!

Lesson 14

Letting Go and Starting Over

by A Student of Life

It is the darkest hour of your life. The unthinkable has happened—your husband of 25 years has left you. Loneliness, inadequacy, and desperation are just some of the negative feelings that cloud your mind. You sit by the phone, hoping he will call, and then telling yourself you won't talk to him if he does. Your hundredth crying jag since he left only sharpens the pain.

Fortunately, there is a light at the end of the tunnel for anyone who has experienced the breakup of a relationship or any other personal setback. A new life awaits you after you have closed the chapter on the old one you left behind. Your new beginning starts with one step: *letting go.*

It's human nature to agonize over our failures. This is especially true with romances and marriages. We hang on to misery and believe that if we keep suffering, the relationship won't end. We will do anything to hang on. But if you have reached this turning point on the road of life, you need to accept that it's over. It probably ended long ago, and you are just now catching up with the news.

Letting go isn't easy. It is hard work, and it's painful. First, you must let go of the negative feelings casting a dark shadow over your life. Let go of the anger, the despair, and the depression. These feelings do not help you get over a relationship and move on—they tie you to the failed relationship and can only hurt you. Forgive yourself for what you might have done wrong or failed to do. Know and accept what you cannot change, and make the conscious decision to move on with your life.

Feeling Good Inside and Out

Besides healing inside and feeling better emotionally, you must feel good about your appearance. Sitting home all day in your bathrobe won't make you feel good about yourself. Even if you don't have a job to focus on, force yourself to get up every day—shower and dress just as you would if you had somewhere to go.

Exercise is important to your well-being on every level—physical, emotional, and spiritual. You don't have to join a gym or run a marathon to get exercise. An exercise regimen can be a walk in the park or on the beach. But do it every day. Some days you won't feel like exercising, but it is healthy habit, and healthy for you, so you should do it. You will feel much better afterward.

Diet is another area we often neglect when we are feeling blue. Avoid caffeine, alcohol, and cigarettes. They will give you a temporary feel-good boost but may make you feel worse. They pick you up and then drop you back down, often lower than you were before. If you have too much stress in your life now to kick an addictive habit, reduce your intake. Later, when you are stable and positive, you can quit smoking or give up coffee.

Eating right is essential to maintain a healthy body. A multi-vitamin and mineral complex can be a smart choice. If you don't feel like cooking for yourself, invite a friend for dinner or go out to eat.

Friendships

If you've experienced a recent breakup, you likely feel quite alone. But you are not alone. Your friends and loved ones can help you through this difficult time. When they offer to help, take them up on it. Avoid people who don't have a positive outlook on life. And when you are with friends, avoid dwelling on your problems. Even a best friend will tire of hearing your latest dramas. Changing the subject to one that interests you both will give you a starting point for a mutually rewarding conversation, and it will make you feel better. Call a friend and make contact with the outside world at least once a day.

Creativity

Begin a creative project. It can be anything; for example, a hobby or craft you haven't done in a while. It could be an aspiration you gave up when you married. If you had a dream of becoming a writer, sit down with a pen and paper or your keyboard and start writing a short story. If you loved photography, dig out your camera, go to the beach or mountains, and click away. A hobby or leisure interest might open the door to an exciting life adventure.

If you are a knitter, make and donate a few items to a domestic violence shelter. If you are a gardener, donate time to help spruce up a local conservation area. If you are not in the mood to exercise your creativity right now, go help out at a soup kitchen for the homeless, or volunteer to help an organization for the disabled or the elderly. You will soon learn first-hand there are people with problems far worse than yours.

Improve your mind by taking a course at your local college, or take a course online. Go to your local library and join a reading group. You can stimulate and sharpen your mind in many ways. While you are exploring these interests, you won't be dwelling on your problems. You will find that a few hours or even the whole day has gone by and you haven't thought about your problems once!

When you realize that, unless you are one of a lucky few, your knight in shining armor is just a fairy tale and he's not coming to rescue you, the next step is to believe you can make it on your own. You *can* do it, and you *will* succeed! Once you have achieved that state of mind, things will start falling into place. New doors will open, and new opportunities will come into your life. Affirm to yourself at least once every day:

> "I can do this on my own."

Look to the Future

Listening to music can stimulate your mind and lift your emotions. Don Campbell, author of *The Mozart Effect* (New York: Avon Books, 1997), advises his readers to set aside ten minutes twice a day to listen to classical music. He suggests listening to Mozart and says that string quartets and violin concertos are good for stimulating your intellect and improving your mood.

Be good to yourself. Pamper yourself. If you like cut flowers, buy a bouquet for yourself. And don't fall asleep in front of the TV. Turn off the television, put on some classical music, light a candle, and curl up in bed.

Try aroma therapy. A pinch of lavender on your pillow and a cup of herbal tea before sleep will not only elevate your spirits but help you to relax if you are having trouble sleeping.

Finally, imagine it is your eightieth birthday and you are looking back on your life. What goals did you not accomplish that you hoped to achieve? What dreams did you not fulfill? Take the lemons life has handed you and turn them into lemonade. Now is a good time to begin working to fulfill those dreams.

You can change your life! Take the first step today, and the next steps will be a piece of cake.

Lesson 15

The Courage to Conquer Fear

by Destiny

Fear. It is the one emotion that can turn your day upside down and cause you to pass up wonderful opportunities merely because you are afraid to make a healthy change or to try something new. Fear is a negative, self-perpetuating emotion. If you let it grow, it will overwhelm you. It will freeze you in your tracks and immobilize your every move.

We all have experienced this gripping emotion and allowed it to send us spiraling into confusion or despair. It can take days or weeks for these murky emotional clouds to pass and our lives to return to normal.

Change is the primary driver of fear. We are afraid to make a change, even when we know it would be healthy, because we don't know what will replace what we are changing. We worry our decisions might hurt someone we care about or bring grief to ourselves. We fear the consequences of past actions will catch up with us. And what if our seemingly rational decisions are mistakes? We worry, so we do nothing. We change nothing, even though we are unhappy in our present situation. We march in place, going nowhere.

Make today the day you will overcome fear, banish it to the past, and allow courage to prevail!

Yes, the unknown can be frightening. Fear of the unknown can prevent you from moving forward toward your goals and fulfilling your spiritual destiny. Fear causes stress, which causes physical and emotional dis-ease. But change is inevitable whether you make an effort or not. Everyone and everything around us is changing constantly. Our loved ones and friends grow and change each day. Growth is progress; progress is change. If you resist change, you cannot grow.

Growth is dynamic; the status quo favors inertia. If you resist change because you have let fear paralyze you, others around you will still continue to grow. One day, you'll awaken to the realization: the parade has passed on by, and you have been left behind!

We are all born with a bright, positive light in our minds and souls. Don't let fear of change or your ego dim that light. Rekindle it within you and let it grow. Rather than fighting change, welcome and embrace it. Embark on a positive course and see where the road of life takes you.

Every morning when you wake up, start the day with a few deep, cleansing breaths. Inhale slowly through the nose and exhale slowly through the mouth. Repeat at least four or five times. Then, to get your day going on a positive track, say the following three affirmations out loud:

Morning Affirmation

I affirm that today will be a blessed day full of sunshine!

I affirm that I am full of positive energy and light!

I affirm that I am lucky to be alive in this beautiful world!

When you have finished your meditation, try to spend a few minutes listening to your favorite music before you head out the door. Let the music fill your soul with good vibrations.

At night before retiring, go to your comfort room or sanctuary and perform deep cleansing breaths for five or ten minutes. Add a little love, trust, and affection into your life by visualizing a lime green light in your mind's eye. Let this positive, comforting energy fill your thoughts and bring the day to a close.

Evening Affirmation

I affirm that I hold the key to success in my life!

I affirm that love, peace, and happiness are gifts I will share with the world!

I affirm that life is what I make it, what I want it to be!

Practicing these spiritual exercises daily will make you stronger. You will discover that as you let love and trust take root and blossom in your soul, fear of the unknown will dissipate.

May good health, love, peace and happiness always be with you!

Lesson 16

Calming Mind, Body, and Spirit

by Beverley

In this lesson, we will explore a potpourri of ideas to soothe the body, mind, and spirit. We already have learned and practiced techniques to reduce stress and bring calmness into our daily affairs. Today, I will present several alternative techniques for you to explore. Pick and choose what you need from this collection. Try a different method every few days and see what works best. You might want to print this list and keep it close by so when you feel stressed, you can refer to it and find a spiritual tool to help you cope.

When you try these exercises, be patient and gentle with yourself. If you are living with stress, you don't want to add to it! Start out with physical relaxation. You must relax your body before you can calm your mind or balance your emotions.

Relax your body with: pleasant walks, yoga, gentle stretching, or focused exercises such as rhythm breathing. Another good technique is tightening and then relaxing muscle groups. Start with the face and neck, and work down. The body can't tolerate constant tension; it needs rest and relaxation to function efficiently.

Meditation can be useful for relaxing as well as expanding spiritual awareness. It can include repeating a mantra or prayer as well as visualization.

Getting a good night's sleep can help you make it through the challenges of a new day. Restful sleep heals and renews the body, stabilizes the emotions, and energizes the spirit. Medical science has documented a wide range of detrimental effects that sleep deprivation and poor sleep habits can have on the body and emotions.

Listen to your body. If you experience stress during the day, pause for a minute and take slow, deep breaths. Pay attention to your body's signals. If you notice yourself clenching your fists, jaw or other muscles, consciously will those muscles to relax. If you are gritting your teeth, stretch and relax your neck and face muscles.

In moments of stress and anxiety, we need to calm the mind and focus on what is good for us, not dwell on negatives. To calm the mind: Meditate. Visualize. Pray. Or focus your attention on a calming scene such as a candle or ocean waves.

Have a plan for the day, the month, and the year, and a blueprint for your life. Know where you are going and how you will get there.

Listen to your own thoughts. Deal with the issues troubling you, one at a time. Choose your most pressing concern and take practical steps to solve it.

Listen to the chatter in your mind too: it can provide clues about stresses that are bothering you or beginning to take root.

Calm your spirit. Read books and inspiring articles. Look for websites and other sources of inspiring thoughts online. Do simple, relaxing things that you enjoy and that touch your soul, like taking a walk on the beach, sitting in your garden, or relaxing and listening to quiet music.

Start each day off with a positive affirmation first thing in the morning.

Learn to distinguish between what you can and cannot change. Act where action can make a difference. Avoid wasting energy on situations where your actions won't change the outcome or you have no control.

Set aside at least ten minutes for yourself each day. Realize that these quiet moments are not only healthy but necessary to your physical, emotional, and spiritual well-being.

Discover what makes you smile and strive to do that each day.

Make a list of what calms you and do one or more of these actions as needed. Calming activities might include: watching a beautiful sunset, taking a stroll on a sunny day, curling up in front of a fire with a good book, calling a friend just to talk and laugh.

Listen to your inner voice. Know the health of your soul. Only you know and understand your true feelings. Others know only what you show or tell them.

Ask for help when you need it. Everyone needs a helping hand or a sympathetic ear from time to time.

Help someone. Few things can make you feel as good as lending a helping hand to someone in need. It takes you out of yourself and away from your problems for at least a short time.

Be thankful for what you have.

Give some of these ideas a try, or try them all. Experiment with new ideas of your own, and share these positive techniques with others in need.

Remember that we are all on a journey on the road of life together. Some people have it easier than others; some of us adapt easily, others do not. Each of us is unique, and what works to heal mind, body, and spirit will vary from one individual to another. Have a relaxing journey!

Lesson 17

Stress—How to Cope With It

By Karen

You come home from work feeling like you have been run over by a bus. You can't wait to take off your shoes and relax. Stress! It's an integral part of our modern lifestyle. A certain amount of stress can be motivating, but chronic stress can have harmful effects on you, physically and emotionally.

Stress is the body's adaptive response to dangerous or demanding conditions. The term "stress" refers to a heightened state of mental or physical awareness, or anxiety arising from such a condition. A person facing a threatening situation is likely to experience stress, and it can produce a variety of symptoms, both physiological and psychological. Some medical and emotional disorders also can cause stress responses.

Negative emotions like anger, depression, and fear can produce stress. When these emotions are expressed often or for a period of time, they produce chronic stress. Changes in your home or work environment, arguments with friends, and reactions to bad news are a few of many events that can trigger stress. Several or more stress-inducing factors can be present at the same time, resulting in higher levels of stress. Some stress inducers (such as physical exercise and creativity) are healthy, but prolonged stress from any source, including healthy ones, can be detrimental.

The effects of stress can be complex, but they all involve a group of physiological responses that developed over the course of evolution to help humans respond to danger. When we perceive danger, the pituitary gland releases a substance called adreno-corticotropic hormone. It stimulates the adrenal gland to release epinephrine and other hormones that speed up the heart rate, raise blood pressure and increase muscle tension. These are part of the fight-or-flight response to danger.

Recognizing Stress

The first step in managing stress is learning to recognize stress points or triggers in your life. We all react to stress in different ways, depending on our personality and our emotional makeup. Some people relish change; others fear it. Much of the stress we experience in day-to-day living is related to the degree of control we want to have over events and situations in our lives. People who are less concerned with controlling their environment typically experience less stress.

Many of us don't realize that we are under stress, and some people experience so much stress they come to believe that the "stressed out" feeling is normal. Stress can manifest in physical symptoms that include:

> insomnia
> digestive problems
> irritability
> headache
> unexplained fatigue

Other symptoms of stress include behavioral habits such as nail biting, teeth clenching, hair twirling; and various emotional responses. You may be hypersensitive to criticism or more pessimistic, angry, or resentful than usual. You might feel unappreciated or misunderstood, or you might feel like a victim. Activities you normally enjoy and look forward to doing may seem like a burden.

Sometimes the physiological and emotional changes that you experience from prolonged stress are gradual and go unnoticed until your health, mood, or relationships have deteriorated. Identifying stressors is an important first step in correcting these negative conditions. Another step is to be more accepting of how you react to events. Many of us are self-critical and expect our reactions to fit some preconceived standard.

Possible Reasons for Stress

Family, marriage, work, and emotions can become sources of stress. Life today is filled with stressors, and alas, many cannot be avoided. Sometimes, the best we can do is find ways to cope. To cope effectively, we must recognize both the source of stress and effective methods for dealing with it.

Family: Most families are a complex network of interactions. The typical family unit is a system; hence, each personality interacts with the others and affects the system as a whole. If one person is ill or expresses negative emotions such as anger and depression, it can disrupt the everyday flow of the system.

A family, like the human body, tries to compensate for an organ that is not functioning up to par. Your entire body may be thrown out of kilter by an injury to an arm or leg. A family likewise may be thrown out of kilter and can become dysfunctional as it compensates for one of its members. When this occurs, high levels of stress are likely. Psychologists, family therapists, or religious advisers can suggest ways to deal with these situations.

Relationships: Intimate relationships can be stressful. Two people who have different personalities, histories, needs, and ways of doing things, are trying to live under the same roof and get along from day to day. That's a tall order even under the best of circumstances. One major stress that couples face involves conflicting expectations. Both parties in the relationship bring a set of expectations to the table, and competing expectations can create much conflict. Conflict by its nature is always stressful.

Over the course of a relationship, partners may go through life transitions, such as the death of a parent or other close family member, losing a job, or physical illness. Other stress-inducing events can include moving, childbirth, illicit affairs, sexual incompatibility, and personality conflicts. All these events, and many others, can impact the relationship and cause stress.

Occupational: Work is a major source of stress for many people. Conflicts on the job, dissatisfaction with a supervisor or the job itself, low compensation, fear of losing a job, fear of moving on to a better job, feeling stifled or unappreciated, and competitive interactions with co-workers all create significant stress. The amount of stress can vary, depending on one's personality and the emotional energy invested in each issue.

How We Think

Some people turn mundane events into crises and make mountains out of molehills. They may react to small things with disproportionate feelings and exaggerate an event to match their feelings rather than adjust their feelings to the event. Others individuals who have low stress reactions and remain calm most of the time are better able to cope with adversity and downplay the effects of setbacks and disappointments.

The following questions can help you gain a grounded perspective on events that occur in your life. By understanding their potential impact, you may be able to reduce the amount of stress they cause. Ask yourself:

— What is the worst that can happen?

— What is the likelihood of the worst happening?

— Have I done everything I can to achieve the outcome I desire?

— Will my life change significantly?

— Will I even remember this event in five years?

— How would I advise a friend in a similar situation?

A few helpful affirmations can go a long way to help you manage stress in most situations. These can include refocusing your thoughts as in these examples:

— I need to decide on my goal.

— I need to calm down.

— I'll take a minute or two here to relax.

— My body is telling me it isn't happy.

— What can I do to calm down? Time for a shower!

— Time for a walk around the block.

— I'll do the best I can and let the rest go.

In addition, there are several useful techniques that can help you reduce stress when it develops in your life. The methods described below can prove beneficial when used correctly.

Relaxation Techniques

A wide variety of relaxation techniques are available: auto-hypnosis, progressive muscle relaxation, and some forms of Yoga, to name a few. One method I've found helpful combines several of these processes.

Sit down in a quiet area. Loosen your clothing and get comfortable. Close your eyes and squeeze them shut as tight as you can. Then relax your eye muscles. Do the same for other muscle groups, working down through your body. Clench your teeth and then relax those muscles. Tighten and relax the muscles in your neck, shoulders, arms, fists, chest, back, thighs, buttocks, calves, and feet. Feel the difference between the tensed and relaxed state. Notice the tingling or other sensation that results when you relax. Just be aware of it, you don't have to do anything about it.

As you relax each part of your body, notice your breathing. Breathe slowly and rhythmically until your entire body relaxes. Finally, imagine yourself in a location you find relaxing and tranquil. This might be a secluded beach, your garden, a pristine lake, or a mountain top. We all have our own special place.

Once you have an image in your mind, bring it into focus. Imagine you are actually there. Bring the scene to life in your mind's eye and enjoy it.

Stay in your "place" for about ten minutes. Then, gently refocus your thoughts in the here and now. Open your eyes. You should feel fully relaxed and refreshed.

Breathing Techniques

Deep breathing and rhythm breathing have been used as effective relaxation methods for centuries. Most forms of yoga and meditation as well as athletic exercises have a breathing component. The intake of oxygen cleanses and revitalizes the body and mind.

Breathing exercises are quick and easy to perform. The simplest form of rhythm breathing is to sit quietly and inhale, slow and deep, through your nose. Exhale through your mouth slowly, expelling the stale air from your lungs. Repeat this breathing cycle for a few minutes or more. You will notice a positive, relaxing difference.

Taking a few deep breaths can be relaxing. It can be a quick stress reliever, and you can do it anytime, anywhere, without attracting attention. As your stress subsides, you will be able to handle things in a calmer and more rational manner.

Experiencing a Full Breath

A more advanced (and effective) breathing exercise is described in this section. In normal breathing, it is not necessary to expand the lungs fully; but for purposes of relaxation and meditation, our goal is full, deep breathing. Therefore, it is important to experience how a complete breath feels. This exercise uses the lungs to capacity and extracts more "life force" or *prana* from each breath. Try doing this exercise sitting down, standing, and lying down. Note the results you achieve in the various postures.

> Exhale deeply, contracting the muscles in your belly. Inhale slowly as you expand the abdomen. Continue inhaling as you expand the chest. Continue inhaling as you raise the shoulders up toward your ears. Hold for a few seconds. Exhale slowly in the reverse pattern. Release your shoulders, relax your chest, contract your belly. Repeat.

This exercise requires practice so that your breathing rhythm is smooth and balanced. Limit yourself to three to five breath cycles the first few times you perform the exercise.

Physical Exercise

All forms of exercise have relaxation components and benefits. Getting oxygen into your blood, releasing toxins in your body through perspiration, and increasing the production of endorphins will have a calming effect on you. That is one of the reasons why people should participate regularly in physical exercise.

Meditation

Are you curious about meditation? Do you want to learn more about what it is? You can try it right now! One who meditates focuses their attention on something (usually in a quiet and private place) for up to an hour. During this time, stress is reduced, the mind relaxes and becomes more sensitive, and it is easier to see "the big picture." With practice, meditation can become an effective tool for managing stress.

Meditators focus on one of three things: (1) a phrase, such as *I am relaxed* or *I am a spiritual being;* (2) an object, such as a candle flame or a religious symbol; or (3) breathing.

To try the first method, which is a simple form of *mantra meditation,* choose a phrase before you start. For example, "I am at peace," or "Peace, Love, Peace, Love." Find a comfortable place to sit. Arrange yourself so your spine, neck, and the back of your head are aligned. You can sit in a chair or on a cushion, whichever you prefer. Relax. Breathe. Get centered.

Say your phrase or mantra to yourself (not out loud). Hear it in your mind. Repeat it as a rhythmic chant. Let the rhythm change, faster or slower.

If your attention shifts (it will, but with practice you'll learn to stay focused), bring it back and refocus your thoughts. Do this for ten to fifteen minutes.

What is a *mantra* and what is its source of power? The next lesson provides a short discourse on mantra meditation and how this timeless method can work for you!

Lesson 18

The Power of Mantra Meditation

by Richard De A'Morelli

The word *mantra* comes from ancient Sanskrit. Loosely translated, it means, "that which frees the mind." *Man* in Sanskrit means mind and t*ra* means peace, tranquility. So the purpose of a mantra is to tranquilize or free the mind.

A mantra is a word or phrase consisting of one to seven syllables. It should have a sacred meaning, such as the name by which you know God, or a concept you cherish, such as Peace or Love. The mantra you choose should inspire you. It should strike a chord of awe and elevate your mind to the highest, most enlightened place.

The sound of the mantra is important. It must "feel" right to you. It must strike a harmonious chord in your mind and resonate with your spirit. For this reason, there is no such thing as a universal mantra. The "right" mantra will vary from one person to another.

A mantra can be anything from repeating the words *Peace. Love. Peace. Love* to saying the name of God, or a short phrase from a litany or prayer. Some religions use the name of God as a mantra. In Islam, God is Allah. In Judaism, God is Jehovah, Jahweh, Elohaynu. In the Christian faith, mantras include Jesus Christ, Heavenly Father, and Holy Spirit. In Zoroastrianism, the world's oldest monotheistic religion, God is called Mazda. In Hinduism, many names for God are used as mantras, including Rama, Vishnu, Krishna, Brahma, and Shiva.

"*OM*" is a well-known mantra. Found in various cultures through the ages, it is the resonating tone of the sixth chakra or Third Eye. It is a powerful mantra. It was introduced to Western culture in the 1960s by Maharishi Mahesh Yogi and followers of Transcendental Meditation. Many older hippies nostalgically remember the peaceful chant "OM" mixed with tinkling bells and fragrant temple incense in the air on warm summer nights.

According to ancient tradition, you choose your own mantra, and it remains your mantra for life. It is your special word, the key to the inner sanctum of your soul. It should be kept secret and be known only to you.

During meditation, a mantra is spoken or chanted repetitively. If you are alone, it can be spoken out loud; otherwise, it is repeated silently in the mind. It provides a focal point for your concentration and creates a harmonizing vibration. This, combined with the methods of deep relaxation, rhythm breathing, and visualization, will help you to reach a state of emotional balance. It will instill tranquility, rejuvenate the body, dispel negative thoughts from your mind, and take you to a higher spiritual plane.

The ancient Hindu scriptures known as the Vedas tell us: "Speech is the essence of humanity..." The New Testament Gospel of John in the Bible says: "In the beginning was The Word. And the Word was with God and the Word was God." Thus, the power of the spoken word, or mantra, has been known from the dawn of civilization.

Words are vibrations. Saying a word produces a corresponding vibration. This is the basis of Numerology, a tool used for character analysis based on a person's name. Some words we speak have harmonious vibrations and convey a feeling of stability and peace. Other words have harsh, discordant vibrations and make us edgy when we hear them, although most people don't realize why.

In mantra meditation, we build on the relationship between sacred words and the positive effect their vibrations have on us. Thus, it is important you choose a mantra attuned to your personality, emotions, and inner being.

Properly used, a mantra is a spiritual power tool. By focusing on your mantra and repeating it during the day, you set in motion a positive vibration that permeates mind, body, and soul. This energy can affect your mood and emotions, and even your bodily functions.

An article on Interfaith Meditation published by Interfaith Sanctuary reports: "For more than 25 years, laboratories at Harvard Medical School have systematically studied the benefits of mind/body interactions. This research confirmed that when a person engages in prayer or repetition of a word, sound, or phrase, intrusive thoughts are passively disregarded, and a specific set of physiological changes ensue. There is decreased metabolism, heart rate, rate of breathing, and distinctive, slower brain waves. These changes are the opposite of those induced by stress and are an effective therapy in a number of diseases that include hypertension, cardiac rhythm irregularities, many forms of chronic pain, insomnia, infertility, cancer, and AIDS. The study included repetitive prayers of all main religious traditions."

A mantra works much like a prism or a laser, which takes ordinary light and reconstitutes it. A prism splits light into its various colors that make up the spectrum, while a laser amplifies light, turning it into a more powerful, focused energy. With a mantra, a word spoken repetitively sets a vibration in motion that the mind draws on and reconstitutes into a powerful, positive force. This energy can promote physical healing, instill emotional balance, and create a sense of inner peace. It can guide the mind to the highest levels of spiritual awareness.

The energy that a mantra draws upon is everywhere. In fact, it is a living form of light. This energy is called *prana*, a Sanskrit word that means "life energy." It is the life force that sustains all living things, human, plant, and animal.

Prana can be transferred from one person to another. For example, healers do this, drawing prana from themselves or the universe and directing it into the person being healed. Likewise, you can use prana to heal your own body and mind. Repetitive use of a mantra allows the mind to reconstitute this life energy and magnify its healing qualities. You must use a mantra that harmonizes with your Higher Mind, and you must be adept at relaxation and meditation so that you can focus on your mantra and achieve the desired effect.

Some people who practice mantra meditation may feel a sense of warmth (or coolness) caused by the mantra's effect on the prana.

This is not a cause for concern; it is a natural effect of this meditation practice, especially at the beginning. After a few days, the sensation will subside. Don't become so focused on the feeling that it distracts you from the other benefits you seek from meditation. Just enjoy the feeling as an early sign of inner growth, and then look beyond it for the spiritual discoveries that await you!

When meditating with a mantra, sit quietly in the meditative posture and relax. Begin with conscious relaxation and deep breathing, and then use a simple balancing exercise. Speak your mantra in your mind, and then repeat it out loud if you are alone and can do so without feeling self-conscious. Perform a slow, deep inhalation, and speak your mantra as you exhale slowly. Speak in a natural tone of voice. Say your mantra repetitively and rhythmically, chanting the word or phrase. There is no "right" speed for reciting the mantra. Some days you may chant faster or slower than others. Go with the flow and do what feels right. Your higher mind knows what to do.

Again, inhale deeply. Exhale, chanting your mantra. With each breath, you will drift deeper into a meditative state. Each breath brings you a step closer to the center of your being and the spiritual altar of your Higher Mind. Don't burden yourself with expectations. Proceed calmly and be patient. Your progress and results will vary from day to day.

This short tutorial is only an introduction to mantra meditation and its possible benefits. Entire books have been written on the subject, so there is much more to learn if you wish to pursue it.

Mantra meditation is just one of many tools you can use to improve your life and achieve a state of Whole Being. Many roads lead to this state, and many pathways lead to enlightenment, just as spokes of a bicycle wheel all lead to the same place. Various kinds of meditation, visualization, yoga, and dream programming are just a few of the pathways to discovery you might explore.

Lesson 19

Centering in the Here and Now

by Susan

It has been said that every person has three sides to their personality: who you think yourself to be, who others think you are, and who you really are.

We live in a paradox of free will and destiny, intertwined like the strands of DNA that make up our physical form. Through spiritual awareness, and by living in the now, we gain the power to choose who we are, who we will become, and the life path that we follow. We'll encounter situations in life that we cannot change, such as the death of a loved one and events caused by the actions of others. But we will have many chances to exercise free will in the small and large details of our lives.

Many people today complain that the "magic" has gone out of their lives. They say they are just existing rather than living. They have lost their sense of purpose and have no motivation to get out of bed in the morning. In reality, they have lost touch with the spirituality that slumbers at the core of their being. They are so addicted to the game that the only things they care about are fame and money, and they pursue them relentlessly. One day, however, they realize that fame and money are temporal. They mean nothing when we return to the universe from which we came.

We are not our *doings*. We should not let ourselves be defined or confined by a career or job title. We should not limit our identities to our roles as mother, daughter, teacher, student, friend. Meaningful action comes from "being." We can embrace these roles but also understand they are only limited facets of our whole being.

We are not our *thinking*. Our lives reach out far beyond our thoughts. I have found it helpful to view "consciousness" as a great ocean in which thoughts swirl by like plankton. The mind can identify with this imagery, and we can raise our thinking to a positive level, adapting some thoughts while letting others drift by. We do not have to own or act on every thought we have as we traverse this vast sea. By fine-tuning our awareness, we can harness the mind and use its positive energy to guide our lives. Becoming the "chooser" of our thoughts puts us in touch with a powerful creative force.

We are not our *emotions*—the feelings that flow through us as we react to life's ups and downs. The next time you become angry, take a deep breath, stand back, and just witness the events. Become the Knower who looks on. Watch what happens to that surge of emotions when you *witness* life from that still place within the moment.

I have a plaque above my desk that reads:

> *What lies behind us and what lies before us are tiny matters compared to what lies within us.*
>
> Ralph Waldo Emerson

I loved the analogy in the course about the muddy cup of water poured into a clear pool and the clear cup of water poured into a muddy pool. In meditation, we can take our muddy perceptions from the hustle and bustle of daily life to the clear pool of our spiritual being and be purified, if only for a few precious minutes each day.

Such is the road map to a happy and fulfilling life—choosing to be the master of our destiny, selecting perspective, finding solutions, and infusing *being* into our vexing lives. A difficult task to be sure when we are swimming in problems. But I am ready to take up the task again, after many years of lagging. Climbing to new heights of inner peace and spiritual awareness is a challenge—but the view is worth the effort.

Lesson 20

Something Beautiful for God

by Molly

Agnes Bejaxhiu was born into a loving family of Albanian parents in Yugoslavia in 1910. At the age of 18, she left this sheltered environment to enter the order of the Sisters of Our Lady of Loreto. Later, she was sent to teach in Calcutta. Once there, she experienced a "call within a call" when she saw the poor, unwanted dregs of humanity living on the streets of that overcrowded, impoverished city.

The humble woman who would become known as Mother Teresa and beloved to the world left her order to begin her life's work in the slums. She started by bringing the dying from the streets into shelters where they could pass on in peace and dignity. In 1948, she opened the first school in the Calcutta slums. Some months later, her first recruit arrived, a young Bengali girl, the first of many. In 1950, the Pope approved a new order of the Missionaries of Charity. From Calcutta, they spread across India.

Mother Teresa and her sisters dressed like the poor, in sandals and sari, and lived with them in the midst of the squalor, disease, and misery. The diminutive little mother imbued her sisters with a profound love for God that translated into action: to love the unloved—lepers, the poor, unwanted infants, the dying.

People in the city heard of this work and offered financial support, while some even gave of their time. Malcolm Muggeridge, the renowned author, broadcaster, and skeptic, was asked to do a TV interview with Mother Teresa for the BBC. It was really no different from any other documentary he had done, and the finished work wasn't particularly impressive. It was televised one Sunday evening.

Yet, the reaction was astounding. Money poured into the studio, a few shillings to hundreds of pounds. All the letter writers said similar things: "This woman spoke to me as no one ever has. I feel I must help her." The program was rebroadcast a few months later and garnered the same response. No appeal for funds was made, although Mother Teresa needed more money as her work expanded.

Malcolm saw that she was a unique person, and he was truly impressed with this unassuming nun. He saw that she was the inspirer, the mainspring of this work. One of her favorite sayings was "Yet not I, but Christ liveth in me." She would also maintain that the poor needed food, clothing, and shelter but more than that, they needed to be wanted. She had a place in her heart for them all. They were children of God for whom Christ died, and so all were deserving of love.

When Malcolm was asked to go to Calcutta to make a documentary on Mother Teresa and her sisters, he accepted with alacrity. At first, she was not interested, and she was suspicious of cameras. A persuasive letter from Cardinal Heenan helped. Once she agreed, she gave her full cooperation. She wrote to Malcolm, "If this program will help people to love God more, we will have it. We will do something beautiful for God."

A fifty-minute program would typically take two to three months to film. We were given five days. We traveled in the sister's rickety old ambulance. Part of the work done by the sisters was picking up the dying from the streets and taking them to a building that had been given to Mother Teresa. "There," she would say, "to die within the sight of a loving face. Some do die; others survive and are cared for."

The home was serene and restful. For filming, however, it was quite difficult, as it was lit by small, high-up windows. Ken, the cameraman, was adamant that filming would be impossible because we only had one small, portable light with us, but he finally gave it a try. Some of the footage was filmed outside where patients were resting in the sun. In the processed film, the shots taken inside were bathed in a beautiful, soft light, and the outside scenes were dim. Ken stated that this result was impossible, technically speaking, but Malcolm observed, "I am personally persuaded that Ken recorded the first authentic photographic miracle." Mother Teresa later wrote that she believed the film had brought people to God.

Malcolm found that besides the sick patients, the sisters also cared for children. Many of them were unwanted. Mother Teresa explained, "Some we pick up, some came from the hospital; some we bring from the jail, and some come to us from the police. We never refuse a child. Our way is to preserve life: the life of Christ in the life of the child."

In 1957, five lepers who could not find help elsewhere came to Mother Teresa. Soon, a doctor came to assist. He trained the sisters for leprosy work. Among the lepers were well-educated people, some rich and capable. Yet, because of their disease, they had become outcasts. The sisters helped and befriended them. As new drugs became available, many were cured. For those who were not cured, a town of peace was built on donated land.

Malcolm Muggeridge became firm friends with Mother Teresa, and they corresponded regularly. He found she often used the word "beautiful." When she agreed to do the film, she had written to him, "Let us do something beautiful for God."

The Sisters of Charity have grown. They now work in many countries with large populations of the poor. Malcolm Muggeridge wrote a classic work introducing Mother Teresa to the Western world. It interprets her life through the eyes of a modern skeptic. He called it "Something Beautiful for God." The words and values of this humble sister have helped to alter the attitude of many people in our world.

Lesson 21

Conflict Resolution

by Dixieco

Arguments can be a major source of discord and stress at work, school, and home. You might be called upon to be the peacemaker among family or friends, or you might need to mediate arguments between colleagues in the workplace. We may be sucked into these disputes, even when we try to avoid them. A spat might flare over something as trivial as children sharing a toy, or it may involve contentious issues that affect family harmony.

Because misunderstandings happen so frequently in everyday living and trigger emotions that may give rise to major stress, it is useful to develop skills you can use to help resolve these situations. Meditation is one of the popular terms used today for the art of conflict resolution. To mediate a disagreement, especially if you are involved in it, here are a few helpful pointers.

First, understand that the anger being expressed probably does not reflect how others feel about you but rather is their response to an emotional situation. For example, a child having a tantrum is expressing a spontaneous emotion. Arguing co-workers might take their irritation out on you just because you are in the middle. Don't take it personally.

Second, don't insist on having your way or shouting over others to make your views heard. If you are mediating a dispute between others, don't take sides. Remind all the parties it is important to reach a mutual resolution. Encourage compromise, and let them iron out their differences and find middle ground.

Finally, develop your own coping skills. How do you cope when an angry person confronts you? What steps can you take to resolve a conflict and avoid hurt feelings? Ultimately, you need to find ways to stay emotionally balanced so that you respond to conflicts in positive, constructive ways.

The simple pointers below may help you to develop effective coping skills you can rely on when conflict erupts and in other situations when stress runs high:

Take a series of slow, deep breaths. It will give you time to relax and calm your emotions.

Take a short walk to release anger before it can build.

Jot down what made you or the arguing parties angry so that you can put the situation into perspective.

Write down the desired resolution or outcome. This will keep the goal firmly in your sight so you don't keep arguing just because you are caught up in the emotions of the moment.

The key to successful conflict resolution is how well you use your coping skills. This will set the tone in all your personal and business relationships. Sometimes, all that is needed to diffuse a conflict are a few conciliatory words or a moment of laughter. Don't underestimate the power of laughter; it can heal rifts and provide welcome relief from anger and emotional tension.

When you are called upon to act as the peacemaker, keeping a positive attitude is half the battle. How you react may help calm a situation or inflame it. Here are a few wise sayings to remember:

In with the good air, out with the bad reaffirms the value of deep breathing. This balancing technique can work wonders.

Laughter is the best medicine. It can diffuse almost emotionally charged situation.

Spend a few minutes every day this week reflecting on how you will handle conflict when it occurs in your life. Think about how you can be the peacemaker and maintain your emotional balance and spiritual clarity when the need arises.

Lesson 22

The Art of Creating Happiness

by Wilma

Some of my friends are going through midlife crises. They complain that they have nothing to look forward to but growing old, and life is no longer worth living. When I ask if they have done anything fun lately, they look at me as if I am crazy. In fact, my friends have done nothing but stay at home and dwell on being depressed. Do they enjoy being depressed? Of course not. But they're not motivated to change. Depression has become a way of life, and it will continue to be a dark cloud hanging over them until they do something to change.

Life is what we make of it. If we choose to do nothing, nothing will happen. So, we must consciously choose to take action. The operative phrase here is *consciously choose*. So how do we break the cycle of depression? By making a conscious decision to come up with a plan. When we put the plan into action, we are practicing the timeless science of "creating happiness."

Begin today. The rest will come easy. Ask yourself: What makes you happy? Whether it is shopping, cooking, gardening, skiing, or whatever, acknowledge that it makes you happy and set about creating more opportunities to do it. When are you happy? Or more to the point, when are you most at peace? Whenever that is, acknowledge it and then create more of it. Take time to document your happiness by keeping a journal, and write down these three things every day:

1. Describe one positive thing about yourself or about today.

2. Describe how you created some happiness today.

3. Set a goal to create happiness tomorrow.

Before you sleep tonight, spend ten minutes meditating. Go to your quiet place and relax. Let your mind drift into a tranquil state. As you meditate, breathe slowly and deeply. Inhale through your nose, and exhale through your mouth. Repeat these slow, deep breaths for a few minutes.

When you are fully relaxed, think of one negative condition in your life today and visualize yourself discarding it. Let it go. Pluck it out of your thoughts and discard it. Flood your mind with a purifying white light until the image, feeling, or memory of that condition is washed away. Imagine what life will be like now that you are free from that negative force. Carry this feeling into tomorrow.

Affirmation

Happiness is not a destination...it is a method of life.
Have a great day tomorrow—let it be the first day of a wonderful new life!

Lesson 23

Support: It Really Does Matter

by Susan

One lesson of which I am continually reminded is the importance of support. It is what keeps me from falling into an abyss. My husband has been my mainstay. He has lived through every milestone in my ongoing bouts with depression, yet he has never wavered in his love and support. My mom, while she was alive, was also very supportive.

In spite of all this loving support, I still found myself falling into the gloom of depression and self-pity. Taking this course helped me realize that I am not alone. Also, a recent event in my life had a profound impact on me.

No matter how much we might want to be alone and responsible only for ourselves, we all need someone. In the uncertain and trying moments of our lives when we need support, that "someone" could be a minister, a doctor, a counselor, a family member, or a friend.

I participate in many online discussion groups. Recently, I posted a message to someone; it was a critique of her website. Something I wrote encouraged her to reach out to me. I shared some of the exercises I had learned from the *You Can Change Your Life* workshop with her. The one thing she lacked was someone she could turn to and share her feelings with...someone who could offer her support when she needed it. I am not a psychologist, but I have experienced much of what she was going through, so I shared several of the lessons from the class with her. I got a warm, happy feeling knowing I had encouraged my new friend to verbalize her troubles to me. It was therapeutic for me too. Listening to this gal's problems made me realize mine were nowhere near as vexing.

One day a few weeks later, I was feeling blue. I had been doing my meditations daily, and I'd narrowed down my problems to two areas. I had shared none of this with anyone but my husband, so reaching out to my new friend was a big step for me. But it helped me to verbalize my own problems, and as a result, I began mapping out steps I could take toward a solution. My writings helped my friend, as did sharing my feelings. For the first time in a long time, she was thinking about and caring about someone else. She was not only supportive of my ideas but offered quite a few of her own.

As I reflect on these recent events, I realized that two lost souls had found each other. Though I can't measure how much this friendship has helped her, I have already taken major steps to heal my own psyche. I hope she also will find a resolution to her problems. I will be there to encourage her.

Lesson 24

The Power of Validation

by Penney

Some people are born problem-fixers. Wives and mothers especially have a caring desire to help family and friends solve their problems. They want to make everyone around them happy. But sometimes the well-intentioned desire to "fix things" comes across as meddling and stirs up needless drama and hurt feelings.

Validation is a simple yet effective process we can use to help others solve problems in daily living. It is a technique in which you listen with empathy and understand another person's point of view without feeling the need to change it. By just listening and seeing things from their perspective, you give them a sense that someone cares, and their feelings do matter. They can then work out their own solutions. Or they might move on to more pressing concerns—just having someone acknowledged them and listen to them vent may have been all the help they needed.

Since learning the basic technique of validation, I have applied it many times in my life. It has helped me to develop patience and have less angst towards my family. They no longer feel I don't understand. And I no longer become bogged down in the problems of others, over which I have no control.

Best of all, through the process of validation, I have become a more effective sounding board and helped more than a few people find their own solutions and change their lives for the better!

Lesson 25

I Changed My Life—So Can You!

by Susi

This is not a lesson but rather an eye-opening life experience. I want to share how the class *You Can Change Your Life* actually has changed my life.

A week ago, I was driving on one of the busiest freeways in the United States. As I approached a steep hill, the traffic in front of me slowed. I had just changed into the fast lane and had to brake. To my horror, my foot went all the way to the floorboard. *I had no brakes!* There used to be an emergency lane on this stretch of the freeway, but it had been turned into a carpool lane. Since I had no brakes and nowhere else to go, I pulled into that lane, and my car rolled to a stop. Just as I put my emergency flashers on, I saw a patrol car in my rear-view mirror. Rather than a provoking paranoia, the sight was a welcome relief.

To make a long story short, I was safe, and I did not hit anyone or get hit. But I was shaken to the core. After I had parked, and as I waited for a tow truck, I saw a sight that proved to be calming. In a nearby tree sat several blackbirds, and on the ground getting ready to climb the tree was a squirrel. Suddenly, I was able to take a deep breath, relax, and thank God, who I sometimes forget is with me always.

I was one of those people mentioned at the start of the class who was always depressed. You were so right that this depression is a "familiar feeling" and so hard to let go. But I have let it go. The daily meditations have helped me to a more peaceful retirement, a less stressful marriage, and a more peaceful day-to-day existence.

One thing I wish you had covered in the course is procrastination. This has caused me to feel many times like I was "less than." When I overcome my tendency to procrastinate, I eliminate much of the stress from my life.

The lesson I would share with others is short and simple: Set a goal! Then take steps to achieve it. Consider how great you will feel when you reach your goal. This process is simple yet powerful—it will help you train yourself to act rather than just wishing you could. It will reinforce in your mind the fact that you can overcome inertia and depression. You really *can* change your life!

Lesson 26

The Secret Power of Dreams

by Tanjla

Have you ever had a dream so real and intense that even though you knew it was just a dream, it dominated your thoughts throughout the day? My daughter is three months pregnant and having intense dreams. Part of the reason is the hormonal imbalance as her body changes during pregnancy; but her dreams also hold hidden messages.

In one dream, she had a fungus growing on her arms. She was far from home and her husband wasn't around to help her. A doctor told her that she needed treatment or she would lose the baby. She couldn't find her husband anywhere; he was gone just when she needed him.

There are several ways to interpret this dream. One is fear of pregnancy and apprehension that something might happen to the baby. Another is fear of desertion once the baby is born, and fear of being responsible for raising a child alone. A third possibility is that my daughter may feel neglected by her husband's busy schedule—he is working two jobs to buy things for the baby and pay the bills so she won't have to work after she gives birth. If all dreams were clear and simple to interpret, we wouldn't have to wonder what our subconscious mind is trying to tell us. But it's not usually that easy.

What happens in your dreams is rooted in your subconscious mind and points to some aspect of your life that needs to be examined closer. For example, a dream about your car breaking down could be warning that you are at risk of getting sick if you keep pushing yourself at a hectic pace.

What if you have the same dream again and again, perhaps even more vividly each time it occurs? I have had a recurring dream through most of my life about being in a big, rambling house. I love houses; I love design. I love the romance of a large, old house. When I dream of this house, I go from room to room, never knowing where I am heading. Sometimes the room turns into a hotel with many people and many hallways. Often, there is an elevator I ride, and I get off on a mezzanine that resembles a department store I visited as a child. Sometimes I wander into a library with hundreds of books and the musty smell of old furniture.

I often have this dream when my life is in transition. The rooms in the house represent problems or emotions I need to deal with. The hotel rooms are the feeling of not belonging anywhere and being in upheaval. The mezzanine is a longing for my youth, when I didn't have to worry much and everything was provided for me. The library is a secret fear that I have much to learn and no time to learn it. The elevator taking me to different floors of my "house" is my fear of not knowing where to turn or where I am going. This dream has been a "comfort dream" throughout my life, and when I couldn't depend on anything or anyone but myself, I would revisit it. I was secure in my own house...in my own body.

Lucid Dreaming

Lucid dreaming is a skill that can be learned. It refers to a state of being aware you are dreaming and being able to control the outcome. This can have benefits in your waking life. For example, say you encounter a frightening creature or circumstance. You realize you are dreaming, and you can choose to wake up—or you might decide to face your fears and confront the situation, knowing whatever happens is only a dream and cannot harm you.

Lucid dreaming can help change you from a helpless victim in waking life to a confident, self-assured person in control of any situation that occurs in your day-to-day existence.

In 1890, after struggling to discover the structure of the benzene molecule, the great professor Friedrich August Kekulé had a dream in which he saw atoms swirling around. Some atoms combined into larger structures, and some looked like snakes. He then observed one of these snakes swallowing its own tail. He awoke and wrote the closed chain or ring theory, which is essential to benzene's composition. Later, at a conference, Kekule announced to his colleagues, "We must all learn how to dream!"

There have been numerous accounts of authors whose dreams led them to write future novels. Robert Louis Stevenson was a prolific dreamer who trained himself to remember his nocturnal adventures. He even wrote a book, Across the Plains, in which he describes how entire stories came to him in dreams. One of his most disturbing dreams resulted in his now famous classic, Dr. Jekyll and Mr. Hyde.

Even if you only use dreams to increase your own self-awareness, they are a natural resource of learning and inspiration.

For the next month, try to be aware of your dreams. Before you go to sleep at night, do a meditation and ask for full recall and understanding of your dreams. When you wake up in the morning, write down any dreams you can remember. Keep a pen and notepad by your bed in case you wake from a dream up during the night.

When you look over your notes, study the wording for clues on how your dreams may be influencing your life or reflecting your current stresses, fears, and desires. Your dreams are the language of your subconscious—try to learn from them!

Lesson 27

Making Choices

by Brenda

Life is full of choices, and the quality of our lives will depend on the choices we make. There is no such thing as "good luck" or "bad luck." We must make the right choices to achieve the good things we want in life. How we make those decisions is what sets us apart from one another and determines our happiness or lack of it.

To make correct life choices, we must consciously take the time and effort to explore our options. We need to weigh the pros and cons, and make wise judgments. We can do this by relying on the tools in these lessons and understanding that, we do have choices.

Here a few steps you can take in day-to-day existence to improve the clarity of your thinking and stay balanced so you can seize upon life's wonderful opportunities as they appear.

Select positive quotes that mean something to you and read them often.

Choose an affirmation (a word or phrase you can say out loud or in your thoughts) that will give you confidence and create a sense of inner peace.

Notice your breathing as you go through your day. With rhythm breathing, you can calm yourself, dispel anger, and put yourself in a relaxed state whenever desired.

Create your own space. It can be a corner of a room or anywhere you can get away from noise and distractions. Make it a place of tranquility—your spiritual sanctuary. Have candles, incense, quiet music, mementos, or anything that can help create a mood of comfort and serenity for you. Spend time daily in your space to pray or meditate.

Many good books are available to help you improve your meditation time. Experiment to find the method that works best for you. The goal of meditation is to focus on a thought, mantra, etc. until your mind is at peace. You will then be "open" to positive energy and thoughts.

Visualization exercises can help you make the right life decisions. At the end of your meditation, visualize what you want to happen, and see the results clearly in your mind.

Don't be a pessimist always fearing things won't turn out right or you will make a mistake. Be positive and expect the best possible results.

Rely on past experience. Think about what has worked for you before. Recall all the right choices you have made. What did you do then? What can you do now in your life to make positive choices?

Don't dwell on past mistakes. Move forward each day, and say this affirmation every morning when you awaken:

Each day is a new beginning!

Lesson 28

Out From the Heart

*I*N THIS LAST LESSON, I would like to share a short work written by James Allen, a British philosopher and author of inspirational books in the early twentieth century. He is best known for his classic, *As a Man Thinketh*, published in 1903, and although his name may be unfamiliar to many readers, Allen is widely credited as the grandfather of the modern self-help and motivational movement. His message of self-empowerment through positive thinking spread around the world and influenced the writings of many prominent authors and their self-help books, including Norman Vincent Peale's *The Power of Positive Thinking* and Joshua Liebman's *Peace of Mind*.

Born on November 28, 1864 in Leicester, England, Allen's early years were marred by tragedy. Soon after he was born, his father's business failed. In 1880, his father moved to America to start a new life, planning to send for his family once he was established. Two days after he arrived in New York, he was robbed and murdered.

The death of Allen's father drove the family into hard times. At fifteen, Allen dropped out of school, and he spent the next twenty years laboring at clerical jobs. But in 1902, he quit his job to pursue writing—an improbable dream for a high school dropout with no education. In leaving behind the security of a paycheck and embarking on a path that seemed doomed to failure, Allen put his faith in the power of the mind and his belief that every human being has free will, and that we are the architects of our destiny.

Allen achieved his goal of becoming a published author. Over the next nine years, he wrote twenty-one inspirational books, all of which are now regarded as classics. That feat in and of itself should be grist for inspiration—if you dream it and believe you can do it, all things are possible.

After publishing his first book, *From Poverty to Power*, Allen moved to Ilfracombe, a scenic seaside town on the coast of southern England. The rolling hills, cobblestone lanes, and Victorian homes dotting the shoreline provided the tranquil setting he needed for his spiritual contemplation and writing.

Not long after he settled on the English coast, Allen began writing his second book, *As a Man Thinketh*. But he was not happy with his first drafts, and it took months of encouragement from his wife, Lily, before he sent the manuscript off to a publisher. It would become his most enduring success, reflecting his views on life and the human yearning to understand our purpose in the Universe.

James Allen lived the modest, ascetic life of a mystic as depicted in the writings of Russian novelist and philosopher Leo Tolstoy, whom he idolized. He followed a path of moderation, self-discipline, respect for all living things, and voluntary poverty. Like Tolstoy, Allen focused on life's most profound aspirations: to be happy, to live in the present, and to find the silver lining in every cloud. An avid learner, he cherished knowledge, welcomed new ideas, and embraced manual labor. He was grateful for the good things that life bestowed on him, no matter how small, and he followed his own teachings on positive thought and action.

A typical day began at dawn with a walk through the rocky hills overlooking the sea. Allen would meditate for an hour and spend the rest of the morning writing. His afternoons were devoted to gardening, and in the evenings, he engaged in deep conversations with friends, admirers, and students of life who traveled from around the world to discuss his writings.

One of Allen's friends described him as "a frail-looking little man, with a mass of flowing black hair. I recall him in the black, velvet suit he always wore in the evenings. He would talk quietly to a small group of us—English, French, Austrian, and Indian—of meditation, of philosophy, of Tolstoy or Buddha, and of killing nothing, not even a mouse in the garden."

Allen's writing career ended abruptly. Just nine years after his first book was published, he died in his sleep at the age of 48. After his death, his wife Lily recalled that "He wrote when he had a message, and it became a message only when he had lived it out in his own life and knew it was good."

James Allen was the proverbial "messenger with the right message for the right time." His writings emerged as the strict doctrines of Protestantism in Europe had begun to soften. Offering an uplifting philosophy of hope that blended Christianity with the mystical teachings of the East, he looked beyond the harsh doctrine that man is born, lives and dies in sin, and is doomed to suffer in the purgatory of Earth. Instead, he offered a benevolent alternative—an optimistic view that man is inherently good, and the seeds of divine wisdom dwell within us all.

James Allen blended traditional Western philosophy and Eastern mysticism into an inspiring message of hope. The ideas expressed in his writings are not original, which is not a surprise, as Ecclesiastes 1:9 reminds us: "There is nothing new under the sun." Allen draws from a variety of sources, especially Buddhism. For instance, *The Dhammapada*, a Buddhist scripture from the third century B.C., tells us, "All we are is the result of what we have thought," and Allen writes, "As a man thinketh in his heart, so is he."

Today, Allen's enduring advice reminds us that even in a world torn by injustice, bigotry, poverty, and strife, we can make a conscious choice to live peaceful, harmonious lives, and to do so, we need only commit to expressing positive thoughts and actions in our daily affairs. He writes: "Yes, humanity surges with uncontrolled passion, is tumultuous with ungoverned grief, is blown about by anxiety and doubt. Only the wise man whose thoughts are pure and controlled makes the winds and the storms of the soul obey him."

I hope that you will enjoy this brief, inspirational missive by James Allen presented in these next pages, and that it will open your eyes and heart to the infinite power and brightest potential of the human mind.

Confucius said: "The perfecting of one's self is the fundamental base of all progress and of all moral development." A maxim as profound and compensable as it is simple, practical, and uninvolved, for there is no surer way to knowledge, nor better way to help the world than by perfecting one's self. Nor is there any nobler work or higher science than that of self-perfection. He who studies how to become faultless, who strives to be pure-hearted, who aims at the possession of a calm, wise, and seeing mind, engages in the most sublime task that man can undertake, and the results of which are perceptible in a well ordered, blessed and beautiful life.

James Allen

1. The Heart and The Life

AS THE HEART, SO IS THE LIFE. The within is ceaselessly becoming the without. Nothing remains unrevealed. That which is hidden is but for a time; it ripens and comes forth at last. Seed, tree, blossom, and fruit are the fourfold order of the universe. From the state of your heart proceed the conditions of his life. Your thoughts blossom into deeds; and your deeds bear the fruit of character and destiny.

Life is ever unfolding from within, revealing itself to the light, and thoughts engendered in the heart must ultimately reveal themselves in words, actions, and things accomplished.

As the fountain from the hidden spring, so flows forth your life from the secret recesses of your heart. All that you are and do is generated there. All that you will be and do will take its rise there.

Sorrow and happiness, suffering and enjoyment, fear and hope, hatred and love, ignorance and enlightenment, are nowhere but in the heart. They are solely mental conditions.

You are the keeper of your heart; the watcher of your mind; the solitary guard of your citadel of life. As such, you can be diligent or negligent. You can keep your heart more and more carefully. You can more strenuously watch and purify your mind and guard against thinking unrighteous thoughts—this is the way of enlightenment and bliss. Or you can live loosely and carelessly, neglecting the supreme task of rightfully ordering your life—this is the way of self-delusion and suffering.

Once you realize that life in its totality proceeds from the mind, the way of blessedness is opened up to you! For you will then discover that you possess the power to rule your mind, and to fashion it in accordance with your Ideal. So, will you choose to strongly and steadfastly walk those pathways of thought and action which are altogether excellent. To you, life will become beautiful and sacred; and sooner or later, you will put to flight all evil, confusion, and suffering. For it is impossible for you to fall short of liberation, enlightenment, and peace, if you diligently guard the gateway of your heart.

2. The Nature and Power of Mind

MIND IS THE ARBITER of life. It is the creator and shaper of conditions, and the recipient of its own results. It contains within itself both the power to create illusion and to perceive reality. Mind is the infallible weaver of destiny. Thought is the thread, good and evil deeds are the foundation, and the web, woven upon the loom of life, is character. Mind clothes itself in garments of its own making.

You, as a mental being, possess all the powers of mind, and you are furnished with unlimited choice. You learn by experience, and you can accelerate or slow down your experience. You are not arbitrarily bound at any point, but you have probably bound yourself at many points. And having bound yourself you can, when you choose, liberate yourself.

You can become bestial or pure, ignorant or noble, foolish or wise, just as you choose. You can, by reoccurring practice, form habits; and you can, by renewed effort, break those habits. You can surround yourself with illusions until Truth is completely lost, and you can destroy each of those illusions until Truth is entirely recovered. Your possibilities are endless; your freedom is complete.

It is the nature of the mind to create its own conditions, and to choose the states in which it shall dwell. It also has the power to alter any condition, to abandon any state. This it is continually doing as it gathers knowledge of state after state by repeated choice and exhaustive experience.

Inward processes of thought make up the sum of character and life. You can modify and alter these processes by bringing will and effort to bear upon them. The bonds of habit, failure, and sin are self-made and can only be destroyed by one's self. They exist nowhere but in your mind; and although they are directly related to outward things, they have no real existence in those things.

The outer is molded and animated by the inner, and never the inner by the outer. Temptation does not arise in the outer object, but in the lust of the mind for that object. Nor do sorrow and suffering belong by nature to the external things and happenings of life, but in an undisciplined attitude of mind toward those things and happenings.

The mind that is disciplined by Purity and fortified by Wisdom avoids all those lusts and desires which are forever bound up with affliction, and so arrives at enlightenment and peace.

To condemn others as evil, and to curse at outside conditions as the source of evil, increases and does not lessen, the world's suffering and unrest. The outer is but the shadow and effect of the inner, and when the heart is pure all outward things are pure.

All growth and life are from within outward. All decay and death are from without inward. This is the universal law. All evolution proceeds from within. All adjustment must take place within. If you cease to strive against others and employ your powers in the transformation, regeneration, and development of your own mind, you will conserve your energy and preserve yourself. And as you succeed in harmonizing your own mind, you will lead others by your thoughtfulness and charity into a like blessed state.

The way of enlightenment and peace is not gained by assuming authority and guidance over the minds of others, but by exercising a lawful authority over your own mind, and by guiding yourself in pathways of steadfast and lofty virtue.

Your life proceeds from your heart and your mind. You have shaped your mind by your own thoughts and deeds. It is within your power to refashion your mind, for better or worse, by your choice of thought. In this manner, you can transform your life and become the architect of your destiny. Let us see how this is to be done.

3. Formation of Habit

EVERY ESTABLISHED MENTAL CONDITION is an acquired habit, and it has become such by continuous repetition of thought. Despondency and cheerfulness, anger and calmness, covetousness and generosity—indeed, all states of mind are habits built up by choice, until they have become automatic. A thought constantly repeated will sooner or later become a fixed habit of the mind, and from those habits proceeds your life.

It is in the nature of the mind to acquire knowledge by the repetition of its experiences. A thought which is, at first, very difficult to hold and dwell upon, at last becomes, by constantly being held in the mind, a natural and habitual practice.

A young person, when commencing to learn a trade, cannot even handle his tools right, much less use them correctly. But after long repetition and practice, he plies them with perfect ease and consummate skill. Likewise, a state of mind, at first apparently incapable of realization, is, by perseverance and practice, at last acquired and built into the character as a natural and spontaneous condition.

In this power of the mind to form and reform its habits and its conditions is contained the basis of a person's salvation. It is the open door to perfect liberty by the mastery of self. For as you have the power to form harmful habits, so you equally have the same power to create habits that are essentially good. And here we come to a point that needs some clarifying, and which calls for deep and earnest thought on your part as my reader.

It is commonly said that it is easier to do wrong than right, to sin than to be holy. Such a condition has come to be regarded, almost universally, as a self-evident truth. Even the great teacher Buddha has said: "Bad deeds, and deeds hurtful to ourselves, are easy to do; what is beneficial and good, that is very difficult to do."

As for humanity generally, this is true, but it is only true as a passing experience, a fleeting factor in human evolution. It is not a fixed condition of things. It is not the nature of an eternal truth. It is easier for us to do wrong than right, because of the prevalence of ignorance—because the true nature of things, and the essence and meaning of life, are not understood.

When a child is learning to write, it is very easy to hold the pen wrongly, and to form letters incorrectly, but it is painfully difficult to hold the pen and to write properly. This is because of the child's ignorance of the art of writing, which can only be dispelled by persistent effort and practice, until, at last, it becomes natural and easy to hold the pen correctly, and difficult, as well as altogether unnecessary, to do the wrong thing.

It is the same in the vital things of mind and life. To think and do rightly requires much practice and renewed effort. But the time will come when it becomes habitual and easy to think and do rightly, and difficult, as it is then seen to be altogether unnecessary, to do that which is wrong.

Just as an artisan becomes, by practice, accomplished in his craft, so you can become, by practice, accomplished in goodness and constructive thoughts and deeds. It is simply a matter of forming new habits of thought. And those to whom right thoughts have become easy and natural, and wrong thoughts and acts difficult to do, have attained to the highest virtue, to pure spiritual knowledge.

It is easy and natural for people to sin because they have formed by incessant repetition, harmful and unenlightened habits of thought. It is very difficult for the thief to refrain from stealing when the opportunity occurs, because he has lived so long in covetous and greedy thoughts.

But such difficulty does not exist for the honest man who has lived so long with upright and honest thoughts. He has thereby become so enlightened as to the wrong, folly, and fruitlessness of theft, that even the remotest idea of stealing does not enter his mind. Sin, or thoughts and actions that have destructive outcomes and effects, can take many forms, of which theft is just one, and I have used this example to more clearly illustrate the force and formation of habit. But all sins and virtues are formed in the same way.

Anger and impatience are natural and easy to a great many people today, because those individuals are constantly repeating angry and impatient thoughts and acts. And with each repetition, the habit is more firmly established and more deeply rooted.

Calmness and patience can become habitual in the same way—by first grasping through effort, a calm and patient thought, and then continuously thinking it, and living in it, until "use becomes second nature," and anger and impatience pass away forever. It is in this manner that every harmful and negative thought may be expelled from the mind; that every hurtful act may be destroyed; that every sin may be overcome.

4. Doing and Knowing

REALIZE THAT YOUR LIFE, in its totality, proceeds from your mind. Realize that the mind is a combination of habits which you can, by patient effort, modify to whatever extent you wish, and over which you can thus gain complete ascendancy, mastery, and control. At once, you will have obtained possession of the key that will open the door to your complete freedom from strife and suffering, and to your enlightenment.

But freedom from the ills of life (which are the ills of your mind) is a matter of steady growth from within, and not a sudden acquisition from without. Hourly and daily must you train your mind to think positive and wholesome thoughts, and adapt right and dispassionate attitudes under those circumstances in which it is prone to fall into wrong and passion. Like the patient sculptor upon his marble, the aspirant to the Right Life must gradually work upon the crude material of his mind until he has wrought out of it the Ideal of his holiest dreams.

In working toward such supreme accomplishment, it is necessary to begin at the lowest and easiest steps, and proceed by natural, progressive stages to the higher and more difficult. This law of growth, progress, evolution, and unfoldment, by gradual and ever ascending stages, is absolute in every aspect of life, and in every human accomplishment. When it is ignored, total failure will result.

In acquiring education, in learning a trade, or in pursuing a business, this law is fully recognized and minutely obeyed by all. But in acquiring Virtue, in learning Truth, and in pursuing the right conduct and knowledge of life, it is unrecognized and disobeyed by nearly all. Hence Virtue, Truth, and the Perfect Life remain unpracticed, unacquired, and unknown.

It is a common error to suppose that the Higher Life is a matter of reading, and learning theological or metaphysical hypotheses, and that Spiritual Principles can be understood by this method. The Higher Life is higher living in thought, word, and deed, and the knowledge of those Spiritual Principles which are imminent in human beings and in the universe can only be acquired after long discipline in the pursuit and practice of Virtue.

The lesser must be thoroughly grasped and understood before the greater can be known and understood. Practice always precedes real knowledge.

The schoolmaster never attempts to teach his pupils the abstract principles of mathematics at the start. He knows that such a method of teaching would be in vain, and learning impossible. He first places before the students a simple sum, and, having explained it, leaves them to do it. When, after repeated failures and ever renewed effort, they have succeeded in doing it correctly, a more difficult task is set before them, and then another and another. It is not until the pupils have, through many years of diligent application, mastered all the lessons in arithmetic, that he attempts to unfold to them the underlying mathematical principles.

In learning a trade, say that of a mechanic, a boy is not at first taught the principles of mechanics, but a simple tool is put in his hand and he is told how to use it properly. He is then left to do it by effort and practice. As he succeeds in plying his tools correctly, more and more difficult tasks are set before him, until after several years of successful practice, he is prepared to study and grasp the principles of mechanics.

In a properly governed household, the child is first taught to be obedient, and to conduct himself properly under all circumstances. The child is not even told why he must do this, but is commanded to do it. Only after he has far succeeded in doing what is right and proper, is he told why he should do it. No father would attempt to teach his child the principles of ethics before exacting from him the practice of family duty and social virtue.

Thus, practice ever precedes knowledge even in the ordinary things of the world; and in spiritual things, in the living of the Higher Life, this law is rigid in its demands.

Virtue can only be known by doing, and the knowledge of Truth can only be arrived at by perfecting oneself in the practice of Virtue. To be complete in the practice and acquisition of Virtue is to be complete in the knowledge of Truth.

Truth can only be arrived at by daily and hourly doing the lessons of Virtue, beginning with the simplest, and passing on to the more difficult. A child patiently and obediently learns his lessons at school by constantly practicing, diligently exerting himself until all failures and difficulties are surmounted. Likewise does the child of Truth, undaunted by failure and made stronger by difficulties, apply himself to the right doing of thought and action. As he succeeds in acquiring Virtue, his mind unfolds itself in the knowledge of Truth, and it is a knowledge in which he can securely rest.

5. First Steps in the Higher Life

SEEING THAT THE PATH of virtue is the Path of Knowledge, and that before the all-embracing Principles of Truth can be comprehended, perfection in the more lowly steps must be acquired, how, then, shall a disciple of Truth begin?

How shall one who aspires to the righting of his mind and the purification of his heart learn the lessons of Virtue? How does he thus build himself up in the strength of knowledge, banishing ignorance and the ills of life? What are the first lessons, the first steps? How are they learned? How are they practiced? How are they mastered and understood?

The first lessons consist of overcoming the wrong mental conditions that are most easily eradicated and are the common barriers to spiritual progress, as well as practicing the simple domestic and social virtues. TO help further your understanding, I have grouped and classified the first ten steps in three lessons as follows:

First Lesson: Discipline of the Body
1st step: Idleness, laziness or indolence
2nd step: Self-indulgence or gluttony

Second Lesson: Discipline of Speech
3rd step: Slander
4th step: Gossip and idle conversation
5th step: Abusive and unkind speech
6th step: Frivolity or irreverent speech
7th step: Critical, captious or fault-finding speech

Third Lesson: Discipline of Tendencies
8th step: Unselfish performance of duty
9th step: Unswerving rectitude or moral integrity
10th step: Unlimited forgiveness

The two vices of the body, and the five of the tongue, are so called because they are manifested in the body and tongue. Also, by classifying them in this manner, it will be clearer to the reader. But it must be clearly understood that these vices arise primarily in the mind, and are wrong conditions of the heart worked out in the body and the tongue.

The existence of such chaotic conditions is an indication that the mind is altogether unenlightened as to the real meaning and purpose of life, and their eradication is the beginning of a virtuous, steadfast, and enlightened life.

But how shall these vices be overcome and eradicated? By first, and at once, checking and controlling their outward manifestations and by suppressing the wrong act. This will stimulate the mind to watchfulness and reflection until, by repeated practice, it will come to perceive and understand the dark, unhealthy, and erroneous conditions of mind, from which such acts spring. The mind will then abandon them entirely.

It will be seen that the first step in the discipline of the mind is the overcoming of indolence or laziness. This is the easiest step, and until it is accomplished, the other steps cannot be taken. Clinging to indolence constitutes a complete barrier to the Path of Truth. Indolence means giving the body more ease and sleep than it needs; procrastinating; and shirking or neglecting those things and conditions in daily life that require immediate attention.

This condition of laziness must be overcome by rousing up the body at an early hour, giving it just the amount of sleep it requires for healthy recuperation, and by doing promptly and vigorously every task, every duty, no matter how small, as it comes along.

To lie in bed after one has awakened, indulging in ease and reverie, is a habit fatal to resolution of character and purity of mind. One should not attempt to do his thinking at such a time. Strong, pure, and true thinking is impossible under such circumstances. One should go to bed to sleep, not to think, and get up to think and work.

The next step is the overcoming of self-indulgence or gluttony. The glutton eats for animal gratification only, without considering the true end and object of eating. He eats more than his body requires, and craves for sweet things and rich dishes.

Such undisciplined desire can only be overcome by reducing the quantity of food eaten, and the number of meals per day, and by resorting to a simple and uninvolved diet. Regular hours should be set apart for meals, and eating at other times should be rigidly avoided. Suppers should be eliminated as they are unnecessary, and promote heavy sleep and cloudiness of mind.

The pursuit of such a method of discipline will rapidly bring the once ungoverned appetite under control, and as the sensual embrace of self-indulgence is taken out of the mind, the right selection of foods will be instinctively and infallibly adapted to the purified mental condition.

It should be remembered most of all that a change of heart is the main thing, and any change of diet that does not promote this end is futile. When one eats for enjoyment, he is gluttonous. The heart must be purified of sensual craving and gustatory lust.

When the body is well controlled and firmly guided; when that which is to be done is done vigorously; when no task or duty is delayed; when early rising has become a delight; when frugality, simplicity, and temperance are firmly established; when one is content with the food put before him, no matter how plain—then the first two steps in the Higher Life are accomplished. Then is the first great lesson in Truth learned, and thus the foundation of a poised, self-governed, virtuous life is established in the heart.

The next lesson is that of Virtuous Speech, in which there are five orderly steps. The first is overcoming the habit of slanderous speech. Slander is inventing or repeating unkind and evil reports about others, exposing and magnifying the faults of others, and introducing unworthy insinuations. The elements of thoughtlessness, cruelty, insincerity, and untruthfulness enter into every slanderous act.

One who aims at living the right life will commence to check the cruel word of slander before it has issued from his lips. He will then check and eliminate the insincere thought that gave rise to it. He will watch that he does not vilify or defame anyone. He will refrain from disparaging, defaming, and condemning the absent friend, whose face he has so recently smiled into or kissed, or whose hand he has shaken. He will not say of another behind his back what he would dare not say to his face. Thus, coming at last to think sacredly of the character and reputation of others, he will destroy those unwholesome conditions of mind which give rise to slander.

The next step is overcoming of gossip and idle conversation. Idle speech can take the form of talking about the private affairs of others; of talking merely to pass away the time; and of engaging in aimless and irrelevant conversation. Such an ungoverned condition of speech is the outcome of an ill-regulated mind.

One endowed with virtue and who expresses the positive attributes of the Higher Life will bridle his tongue, and thus learn how rightly to govern the mind. He will not let his tongue run idly and foolishly, but will make his speech strong and pure, and either talk with a purpose or remain silent.

Abusive and unkind speech is the next vice to be overcome. The man who abuses and accuses others has himself wandered far from the Right Way. To hurl harsh words and insults at others is to sink deeply into folly. When one is inclined to abuse, curse, and condemn others, let him restrain his tongue and look within himself. The virtuous man refrains from all abusive language and quarreling. He employs only words that are useful, necessary, pure, and true.

The sixth step is the overcoming of levity, or irreverent speech. Light and frivolous chatter; the retelling of crude jokes or vulgar stories; having no other purpose than to raise an empty laugh;

making offensive utterances; using contemptuous and disrespectful words when speaking to or of others, and particularly those who rank as one's teachers, guardians, or superiors—all of this will no longer be spoken by the lover of Virtue and Truth.

Upon the altar of irreverence, absent friends and companions are immolated for the passing excitement of a momentary laugh, and all the sanctity of life is sacrificed to the zest for ridicule. When respect towards others and the giving of respect where respect is due are abandoned, Virtue is abandoned. When modesty and dignity are eliminated from speech and behavior, Truth is lost.

The virtuous will be of earnest and reverent speech. He will think and speak of the absent as he thinks and speaks of the dead—tenderly and sacredly. He will put away thoughtlessness, and watch that he does not sacrifice his dignity to gratify a passing impulse to frivolity and superficiality. His humor will be pure and innocent, his voice will be subdued and musical, and his soul will be filled with grace and sweetness as he succeeds in conducting himself as befits a person who seeks and cherishes Truth.

The last step in the second lesson is to overcome criticism and fault-finding speech. This vice of the tongue takes the form of magnifying and harping on small or apparent faults, of foolish quibbling and hair-splitting, of pursuing vain arguments based on groundless suppositions, beliefs, and opinions.

Life is short and real, and sin, sorrow, and pain are not remedied by carping and contention. The man who is always ready to seize on the words of others in order to contradict and dispute them has yet to reach the higher path of Virtue or the truer life of self-surrender. One who is ever vigilant to check his own words in order to soften and purify them will find the higher way and the truer life. He will conserve his energies, maintain his composure of mind, and preserve within himself the spirit of Truth.

When the tongue is well controlled and wisely subdued; when selfish impulses and unworthy thoughts no longer rush to the tongue demanding utterance; when the speech has become harmless, pure, gentle, gracious, and purposeful, and no word is uttered but in sincerity and honesty—then are the five steps to virtuous speech accomplished, and then is the second great lesson in Truth learned and mastered.

Now some will ask, "But why all this discipline of the body and restraint of the tongue? Surely the Higher Life can be realized without such strenuous labor and such persistent effort?" No, it cannot. In the spiritual as the material, nothing is done without labor, and the higher cannot be known until the lower is fulfilled.

Can a man make a table before he has learned how to handle a tool and drive a nail? And can a man fashion his mind in accordance with Truth before he has overcome the slavery of his body?

As the intricacies of language cannot be understood and wielded before the alphabet and simple words are mastered, neither can the deep subtleties of the mind be understood and purified before the ABC's of right conduct are understood and acquired.

As for the labor involved—does not the youth joyfully and patiently submit himself to a lengthy apprenticeship in order to master a craft? And does he not, day by day, carefully and faithfully carry out every detail of his master's instructions, looking forward to the time when, perfected through obedience and practice, he shall be himself a master?

The aspirant who sincerely aims at excellence in music, painting, literature, or in any trade, business, or profession must be willing and devoted to giving his whole life to the acquirement of that particular perfection. Shall labor, then, be considered where the very highest excellence is concerned—the excellence of Truth?

One who complains, "The Path you have pointed out is too difficult; I must have Truth without labor, salvation without effort" –that person will not find his way out of the confusions and sufferings of selfhood. He will not find the calm, well-fortified mind and the wisely ordered life. His love is for ease and idle living, and not for Truth.

One who, deep in his heart, adores Truth and aspires to know it, will consider no labor too great to be undertaken, and will adopt it joyfully and pursue it patiently. By perseverance in practice, he will come to the knowledge of Truth.

The necessity for this preliminary discipline of the body and tongue will be more clearly perceived when it is fully understood that all these wrong and negative outward conditions are merely the expressions of wrong and negative conditions of the heart. An indolent body reflects an indolent mind; an ill-regulated tongue reveals an ill-regulated mind, and the process of remedying that wrong condition is really a method of rectifying the inward state.

But the overcoming of these conditions is only a small part of what is really involved in the process. The ceasing from evil leads to, and is inseparably connected with, the practice of good. While a you are overcoming laziness and self-indulgence, you are, in fact, cultivating and developing the virtues of abstinence, temperance, and punctuality. You are acquiring the strength, energy, and resolve which are indispensable to the successful accomplishment of the higher tasks. While you are overcoming the vices of speech, you are developing the virtues of truthfulness, sincerity, reverence, kindliness, and self-control, and you are gaining that mental steadiness and fixedness of purpose, without which the more remote subtleties of the mind cannot be regulated, and the higher stages of conduct and enlightenment cannot be reached.

Also, as you do right, your knowledge deepens and your insight is intensified. Just as a child's heart is glad when a school task is mastered, so with each victory achieved, the person of virtue experiences a bliss which the seeker of pleasure and excitement can never know.

Now we come to the third lesson in the Higher Life, which consists of practicing and mastering, in one's daily life, three great fundamental Virtues:

1) Unselfish Performance of Duty
2) Unswerving Rectitude (Moral Integrity)
3) Unlimited Forgiveness

Having prepared the mind by overcoming the more surface and chaotic conditions in the first two lessons, the striver after Virtue and Truth is now ready to enter upon greater and more difficult tasks, and to control and purify the deeper motives of the heart.

Without the right performance of duty, the higher virtues cannot be known, and Truth cannot be comprehended. Duty is generally regarded as an irksome labor, a compulsory something that must be toiled through, or in some way avoided. This way of regarding duty proceeds from a selfish condition of mind, and a wrong understanding of life. All duty should be regarded as sacred, and it's faithful and unselfish performance one of the leading rules of conduct. All personal and selfish considerations should be extracted and cast away from the doing of one's duty, and when this is done, duty ceases to be irksome, and becomes joyful. Duty is only irksome to the person who craves some selfish enjoyment or benefit for himself. Let the person who is chafing under the irksomeness of his duty look closely within, and he will find that his weariness proceeds not from the duty itself but from his selfish desire to escape it.

If you neglect duty, be it great or small, or of a public or private nature, you neglect Virtue. If you, in your heart, rebel against duty, you rebel against Virtue. When Duty becomes a thing of love, and when every duty undertaken is done accurately, faithfully, and dispassionately, there is much subtle selfishness removed from the heart, and a great step is taken towards the heights of Truth. The virtuous seeker concentrates his mind on the perfect doing of his own duty, and does not interfere with the duty of another.

The ninth step is the practice of Unswerving Rectitude or Moral Integrity. This virtue must be firmly established in the mind and enter into every detail of one's life. All dishonesty and deception must be forever put away, and the heart purged of every vestige of insincerity and deception. The least digression from the path of rectitude or righteousness is a deviation from Virtue.

There must be no extravagance and exaggeration of speech, but the simple truth should be stated. Engaging in deception, no matter how seemingly insignificant, for boastful pride, or with the hope of personal advantage, is a state of delusion that one must work to dispel. It is demanded of the seeker of Virtue that he must not only practice the most rigid honesty in thought, word, and deed, but be exact in his statements, always expressing the actual truth.

In thus shaping a person's mind to the principle of Rectitude or moral integrity, he will gradually come to deal with people and things in a just and impartial spirit, putting fairness before himself, and viewing all things with freedom from personal bias, passion, and prejudice. When the Virtue of Rectitude is fully practiced and comprehended, causing all inclination to untruthfulness to cease, then is the heart made purer and nobler. Then is character strengthened and knowledge enlarged, and life takes on a new meaning and a new power. Thus, the ninth step is accomplished.

The tenth step is the practice of Unlimited Forgiveness. This consists of overcoming the sense of injury that springs from vanity, selfishness, and pride; and of exercising charity and generosity towards all. Spite, retaliation, and revenge are so utterly ignoble, so base, and so small and foolish, as to be altogether unworthy of being noticed or harbored. No one who fosters such conditions in his heart can rise above folly and suffering, and set his life aright. Only by casting them away, and ceasing to be moved by them, can a one's eyes be opened to the true way of life. Only by developing a forgiving and charitable spirit can one hope to approach and perceive the strength and beauty of a well-ordered life.

In the heart of the strongly virtuous person, no feeling of personal injury can arise. Such an individual has put away all retaliation and has no enemies. If other people declare themselves as his enemies, he will regard them kindly, understanding their ignorance, and making full allowance for it.

When this state of heart is arrived at, then the tenth step in the discipline of one's self-seeking inclinations is accomplished. Then the third great lesson in Virtue and Knowledge is learned and mastered.

Having thus defined the first ten steps and three lessons in right-doing and right-knowing, I leave those of my readers who are prepared for them to learn and master them in their everyday life.

There is, of course, a still higher discipline of the body, a more far-reaching discipline of the tongue, and greater and more all-embracing virtues to acquire and understand before the highest state of bliss and knowledge can be grasped. But it is not my purpose to deal with them here. I have expounded only the first and easiest lessons on the Higher Path, and by the time these are mastered, the reader will have become so purified, strengthened, and enlightened, that he or she will not be left in the dark as to his future progress.

Those readers who have completed these three lessons will already have perceived, beyond and above, the high altitudes of Truth, and the narrow and precipitous track that leads to them, and will choose whether or not to proceed.

The straight Path described above can be pursued by all with greater profit to themselves and to the world. And even those who do not aspire to the attainment of Truth will develop greater intellectual and moral strength, finer judgment, and deeper peace of mind by perfecting themselves in this Path. Nor will their material prosperity suffer by this change of heart; in fact, it will be rendered truer, purer, and more enduring. For if there is one who is capable of succeeding and fitted to achieve, it is the person who has abandoned the petty weaknesses and vices of everyday living, who is strong enough to rule his body and mind, and who pursues with fixed resolve the path of unswerving integrity and sterling virtue.

6. Mental Conditions and Their Effects

WITHOUT GOING into the details of the greater steps and lessons in the right life (a task outside the scope of this small work) a few hints about those mental conditions from which life in its totality springs seem in order. These hints will prove helpful to those who are ready and willing to penetrate further into the inner realm of heart and mind where Love, Wisdom, and Peace await the rapidly progressing student of life.

All sin is the by-product of ignorance. It is a condition of darkness and undevelopment. The wrong-thinker and the wrong-doer is in the same position in the school of life as the ignorant pupil in the school of learning. He has yet to learn how to think and act correctly, that is, in accordance with Law. The pupil in learning is not happy so long as he does his lessons incorrectly. Likewise, unhappiness cannot be escaped while sin remains unconquered.

Life is a series of lessons. Some people are diligent in learning them, and they become pure, wise, and profoundly happy. Others are negligent and do not apply themselves. They remain impure, foolish, and unhappy.

Every form of unhappiness springs from a wrong condition of mind. Happiness is inherent in right conditions of mind. Happiness is mental harmony, unhappiness is mental inharmony. While a man lives in wrong conditions of mind, he will live a wrong life and will suffer continually.

Suffering is rooted in error. Bliss is inherent in enlightenment. There is salvation for man only in the destruction of his own ignorance, error, and self-delusion. Where there are wrong conditions of mind, there is bondage and unrest. Where there are right conditions of mind, there is freedom and peace.

Here are some of the leading wrong mental conditions and their disastrous effects upon one's life:

1. *Hatred*—which leads to injury, violence, disaster, and suffering.

2. *Lust*—which leads to confusion of intellect, remorse, shame, and wretchedness.

3. *Covetousness*—which leads to fear, unrest, unhappiness, and loss.

4. *Pride*—which leads to disappointment, humiliation, and lack of self-knowledge.

5. *Vanity*—which leads to distress and mortification of spirit.

6. *Condemnation*—which leads to persecution and hatred from others.

7. *Ill-will*—which leads to failures and troubles.

8. *Self-indulgence*—which leads to misery, loss of judgment, disease, and neglect.

9. *Anger*—which leads to the loss of power and influence.

10. *Desire or Self-slavery*—which leads to grief, folly, sorrow, uncertainty, and loneliness.

The wrong conditions of mind above are merely negations. They are states of darkness and deprivation, and not of positive power. Evil is not a power; it is ignorance and misuse of good. The hater is one who has failed to do the lesson of Love correctly, and he suffers in consequence. When he succeeds in doing it rightly, the hatred will have disappeared, and he will see and understand the darkness and impotence of hatred. This is so with every wrong or negative condition.

The following are some of the more important right mental conditions and their beneficial effects upon one's life:

1. *Love*—which leads to gentle conditions, bliss, and blessedness.

2. *Purity*—which leads to intellectual clearness, joy, confidence.

3. *Selflessness*—which leads to courage, satisfaction, happiness, and abundance.

4. *Humility*—which leads to calmness, restfulness, knowledge of Truth.

5. *Gentleness*—which leads to emotional equilibrium, contentment under all circumstances.

6. *Compassion*—which leads to protection, love, and reverence from others.

7. *Goodwill*—which leads to gladness, success.

8. *Self-control*—which leads to peace of mind, true judgment, refinement, health, and honor.

9. *Patience*—which leads to mental power, far-reaching influence.

10. *Self-conquest*—which leads to enlightenment, wisdom, insight, and profound peace.

The right conditions of mind above are states of positive power, light, joyful possession, and knowledge. The good person knows. He has learned to do his lessons correctly, and thereby understands the exact proportions that make up the sum of life. He is enlightened, and he knows good and evil. He is supremely happy, doing only that which is divinely right.

A person who is involved in the wrong conditions of mind does not know. He is ignorant of good and evil, of himself, of the inward causes that make his life. He is unhappy, and believes other people are the cause of his unhappiness. He works blindly and lives in darkness, seeing no central purpose in existence, no orderly and lawful sequence in the course of things.

The seeker who aspires to the attainment of the Higher Life—who would perceive with unveiled vision the true order of things and the meaning of life—let him abandon all the wrong conditions of the heart and persevere unceasingly in the practice of good. If he suffers, or doubts, or is unhappy, let him search within until he finds the cause, and having found it, let him cast it away. Let him so guard and purify his heart that every day less of darkness and negativity and more of good and light shall issue therefrom. So will he daily become stronger, nobler, and wiser. So will his blessedness increase, and the Light of Truth, growing ever brighter within him, will dispel all gloom and illuminate his Pathway.

7. Exhortation

DISCIPLES OF TRUTH, lovers of Virtue, seekers of Wisdom; you, also, who are sorrow stricken, knowing the emptiness of the self-life, and who aspire to a life that is supremely beautiful and serenely joyful—take now yourselves in hand, enter the Door of Discipline, and know the Better Life.

Put away self-delusion. Behold yourself as you are, and see the Path of Virtue as it is. There is no lazy way to Truth. If you seek to stand upon the mountain's summit, you must strenuously climb, and rest only to gather strength. If the climbing is less glorious than the cloudless summit, it is still glorious. Discipline in itself is beautiful, and the end result of discipline is sweet.

Rise early and meditate. Begin each day with a conquered body and a mind fortified against error and weakness. Temptation will never be overcome by unprepared fighting. The mind must be armed and arrayed in the silent hour. It must be trained to perceive, to know, to understand. Temptation and negativity disappear when right understanding is developed.

Right understanding is reached through unwavering discipline. Truth cannot be reached but through discipline. Patience will increase by effort and practice, and patience will make discipline beautiful.

Discipline is irksome to impatient people and the lovers of self, so they avoid it, and continue to live loosely and mired in confusion.

Discipline is not irksome to the lover of Truth, and he will find the infinite patience that can wait, work, and overcome. Just as the joy of the gardener who sees his or her flowers develop day by day, so is the joy of the man of discipline who sees the divine flowers of Purity, Wisdom, Compassion, and Love, grow within his heart.

Those who live loosely cannot escape sorrow and pain. Their undisciplined minds fall, weak and helpless, before the fierce onslaught of passion.

Array well your mind, then, lover of Truth. Be watchful, thoughtful, and resolute. Your salvation is at hand; your readiness and effort are all that are needed. If you fail ten times, do not be disheartened. If you fail a hundred times, rise up and pursue your way. If you should fail a thousand times, do not despair. When the right Path is entered, success is sure if the Path is not abandoned.

First strife, and then victory. First labor, and then rest. First weakness, and then strength. In the beginning the lower life, and the glare and confusion of battle, and at the end the Life Beautiful, the Silence, and the Peace.

> All common things, each day's events,
>   That with the hour begin and end,
> Our pleasures and our discontents,
>   Are rounds by which we may ascend.
>
> The distant mountains, that uprear
>   Their solid bastions to the skies,
> Are crossed by pathways, that appear
>   As we to higher levels rise.
>
> *Henry Wadsworth Longfellow*

--#--

About the Author

"Some write as a hobby, others write for therapy or a career boost, and some have an unquenchable passion for writing in their blood--they are always writing, day and night, at the keyboard, in their heads. It's their obsession. They might be more successful doing other things, but they just want to write. I get that. I've been writing since I was a kid, and I will keep writing until my final breath."

Bestselling author and editor Richard De A'Morelli published his first article in a national magazine at age 14 and signed a multi-book contract with a West Coast publisher at 18. Since then, he has written 25 books, including an English grammar bestseller, two self-help/inspirational bestsellers early in his career, more than a dozen writing courses, and three novels under pseudonyms.

During a five-year stint as a journalist in Southern California, Richard published more than 600 news articles and features under his byline. While working as a reporter, he taught journalism and creative writing at a local community college and at Learning Tree University. A decade later, he went on to design and teach a popular series of online writing courses for Virtual University.

Beyond his writing endeavors, Richard is an elite editor with 35 years of experience editing and publishing books, magazines, and newspapers, both print and digital. He was a by-lined editorial staff member for the late Irving Wallace, and he has held Senior Editor and Managing Editor positions with book and magazine publishers. Affectionately nicknamed "Jedi Editor" by his clients, Richard's recent editing projects include *Apocalypse Orphan*, a 2016 Amazon sci-fi bestseller by Tim Allen, and *Eden's Serum*, an award-winning sci-fi/fantasy thriller by Angelique Anderson.

Richard can be reached through his virtual office and blog at https://richard.spectrum.org/ where links to his social pages on Facebook, Twitter, Instagram, Amazon and LinkedIn can be found.

More Books from Spectrum Ink

As A Man Thinks
Edited by Richard De A'Morelli

This special edition of James Allen's self-help classic, *As a Man Thinks*, explores how the power of thought affects you on every level, and how you can take control of your life and destiny. Your thoughts create every condition in your life, and by changing the way you think, you can change your life, your health, and your destiny. If you've been beset by disappointment and failure, the empowering wisdom in this book will turn your life around. Learn how to use the power of your mind to build confidence, unlock hidden talents, cope with depression and stress, and overcome self-destructive habits to build a bright future and become the architect of a successful, happy life.

Available in e-book, paperback, and hardcover collector's editions, this book retains James Allen's timely wisdom but has been updated to a modern style that is easy and enjoyable to read. Also, the book has been expanded—each chapter includes additional insights and points to remember that will help empower you to change the way you think and thereby change your life.

Buy online at your favorite bookstore or visit the Spectrum Ink website at **https://books.spectrum.org** for further details.

ELEMENTS OF STYLE 2017
by Richard De A'Morelli

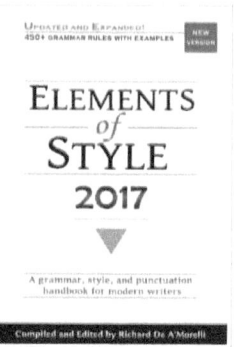

Elements of Style 2017 presents a roundup of grammar, style, and punctuation rules for writers who must edit or proofread manuscripts and other documents as well as students writing academic papers. Loosely based on William Strunk's 1921 grammar classic, *The Elements of Style*, this expanded and fully updated version includes 450+ modern grammar, style and punctuation rules with easy-to-follow examples.

Choose any chapter in this book, follow the practical advice, and you will see an overnight improvement in your writing. Read a chapter a day, and in a few weeks, you will be amazed by the polished quality of your final draft.

• Writers of all skill levels will discover quick and easy ways to fix grammar, style and punctuation errors in their manuscripts.

• Students can use these rules to edit and polish book reports, essays, and other homework. Teachers can use this book to help students learn grammar and punctuation without the tears.

• Employees can follow these simple guidelines in the workplace to produce well-written reports, brochures, and other materials.

Learn how to improve your grammar and style, and take your writing to the next level with Elements of Style 2017.

This book is available in e-book, paperback and hardcover editions. Purchase online at your favorite bookstore or visit the publisher's website at **https://books.spectrum.org** for retail/wholesale availability and ISBN numbers

www.ingramcontent.com/pod-product-compliance
Lightning Source LLC
Chambersburg PA
CBHW020307010526
44107CB00001B/14